D0597194

We're Just Not That Into You

Dating Disasters from the Trenches

Karina Smirnoff

Lindsay Rielly

ISBN (Hardcover): 978-1618688828
ISBN (eBook): 978-1618688835

Published by Post Hill Press
109 International Drive, Suite 300
Franklin, TN 37067

www.posthillpress.com

This book is dedicated to us girls, who still believe in true love and will never stop until we find it, to all the hopeless romantics whose hope drives us to continue kissing frogs in search for the right guy, and to all the frogs who make our love escapades ever so adventurous and entertaining.

To our moms, Nancy and Tatyana for being our most treasured confidantes.

To our dads, Keith and Glen for believing that we are angels and worthy of kings.

And to Royce, our most beloved little boy in the whole world, who is sure to remain the perfect gentleman and make a wonderful husband one day.

Table of Contents

Introduction

Karina

Our date started out in the park—in the little garden area in the middle of it. That's where we met after agreeing to go out that night, and as soon as we said hello to each other, we immediately started holding hands. He was older than I was. He had very dark eyes and dark hair. Misha was his name. He was the envy of many other girls, but he'd asked me out and I was thrilled beyond belief. We talked for a bit, continuing to hold hands, and decided to walk over to the disco for an evening of dancing. It was just starting to get dark. It was summer so the sky was full of stars. My stomach was doing flips as we walked. I had a real crush on this guy.

The *disco* was actually Disco Night at summer camp in the Ukraine—a camp for kids who skated, did ballroom dancing, or practiced gymnastics. I was eleven years old. Since I was a late bloomer (I didn't get boobs until age fifteen or sixteen), this was my first "date" ever. It was a weird thing for me—I'd only ever played with boys, not dated them. And I was a tomboy at that. So when he showed interest in me, I thought: *Wow, this is awesome!* I was terrified, too, but excited to be this guy's summer girlfriend. I felt like I'd won something.

While we were walking into the disco that night, he held my hand, and it felt like a monumental moment. People watched us walk in, and I felt as important as an eleven-year-old girl could ever feel. It was huge. There was no kissing that night. Just dancing and hand-holding, but it was a date for the books. The romance ended when summer did. But I remember it like it was yesterday.

I also remember sharing the details of it with my girlfriends at camp later that night. We talked about it all night when I got home. And so started the lifelong tradition of dissecting every second of every date or encounter with a guy with my girlfriends. I know you can relate. Almost as much fun as the dates are the postmortems with the girls over glasses (sometimes bottles) of wine, especially following those really crazy ones that don't go as expected and provide years and years of laughter with the "Remember that guy who . . . " stories.

These days, I tell the details of my dating life to my best friend Lindsay. And she tells me about hers. As most of you probably know, I'm a pro dancer on *Dancing with the Stars*. Lindsay is my manager. People tell us we look alike, too. Between us, we've had our share of funny, amazing, bad, shockingly bad, and almost unbelievably bad dates. Hundreds of them. So have most of our friends.

One night, as Lindsay and I were having a drink and laughing about yet another tragic and hilarious night out with a guy, we had an idea: Let's collect all of these stories—there are *so* many of them, after all—and put them together in a book. The more people we told, the more interest we had from our friends to participate. It snowballed. We realized that everyone had a great (and by great sometimes we mean terrible) date story they wanted to share. Some of ours are self-deprecating and we're laughing at ourselves along the way, but sometimes, some of the things these guys do, well, you'll be surprised. But maybe you won't be too surprised if you too have dated *The Cheapskate, The Serial Cheater*, and *The Wanna-Be-Straight Guy*.

Don't get us wrong: We love guys. We do. And there are thousands of gems out there worth marrying. We just haven't found one for ourselves yet. In our search, over the years having kissed hundreds of frogs, we both had an epiphany. We used to mostly blame ourselves for being too choosy or dating unavailable guys, but then we realized, most times, we were in the driver's seat. We too can call the shots in our dating lives. And frankly, more often, as we realized how happy we were with our own lives, we were mostly just not that into *them*. At times, the guys were the problem, not us. That realization made it easier for us to laugh off the bad ones and keep a positive attitude as we looked for *the one*.

Lindsay ....

So true, Karina. I think what we realized is that in order to find the right *one* we needed to embrace the process and not be afraid to laugh at ourselves. We both have rich and fulfilling lives. I'm a single mom with an amazing little boy named Royce. He's the greatest human being I've ever met, and I feel so blessed to have him in my life. Neither of us feels we have to settle in the guy department. We're both looking for Mr. Right, but we are okay taking the time to find the man of our dreams. We're successful, and we have great friends and awesome families. And we have each other! So we're taking our time. But wow, do we have some war stories from the dating trenches.

You might be wondering how we have trouble finding our Romeo. The bottom line is that we are just like everyone else. We date duds and awesome guys, just like you do. And fortunately we can laugh about them all—especially the disasters. Karina's celebrity makes it tough sometimes. Guys get immediately infatuated with her beauty—with her sparkle and charisma. She's captivating. They think they know her without knowing her. They get really into her really fast. Sometimes she has to move quickly to figure out if she actually likes them. Often, they have this expectation that she'll be the doting wife type. But she's as driven about her career as they are most of the time, and that's a surprise to some of them. (As you'll soon read, some men have even cried about her working too hard.)

So that's why we wrote this book. Our dating stories are universal. They're just like your stories and your friends' stories—the ones you tell over dinner and drinks or while you're out for a run together. We figured, if people like Karina and I can laugh about dates, you girls can all laugh about yours, too. We crack ourselves up over some of these stories. Over and over, in many cases. And our friends do, too.

So here's to us *all* finding Mr. Right and laughing about it along the way.

XOXO,

Karina and Lindsay

Chapter 1:
Listen to the Signs

Could Anything Else Go Wrong?

Karina

Sometimes the universe tries to tell us something, but we just don't listen. In this instance, the signs couldn't have been clearer. Still, I pushed through, ignoring the blaring, flashing, screaming stream of them, and went on a blind date arranged by a friend. This was back when I was a student at Fordham University in New York.

The date-to-be was in law school. So was my guy friend who set us up. My friend was dorky and there was no chemistry between us, but he said to me one afternoon that he thought I needed to be with someone smart and that his friend was super smart. I agreed because smart is a quality I like in a guy. We were all set to meet in Manhattan, but since I lived in Staten Island, I had a bit of a trek to meet this guy. I had a few choices: 1) public transportation made up of buses, ferries, and subways; 2) drive myself in across the Verrazano Bridge through Brooklyn; 3) drive to the train station and go from there. I chose the last option and hopped in my old car to make the journey. It was a dark burgundy clunky old Buick LeSabre—the first car I ever had. It had dull red seats inside. A family member had given it to me.

It seemed like a good idea at the time to drive part of the way, mostly because I wouldn't be flustered from the trip. I was wearing my one really hot pair of heels. These were my going-out shoes. They were closed-toe super high pumps with that rubbery late-'90s platform in off-white. I was putting myself through college working as a paralegal, so I didn't have extra money for five thousand pairs of shoes. These were my one and only pair of statement shoes—brand name Dolce & Gabbana. I wore a super tight, light brown pencil-skirt type dress with a little jacket over the top. It certainly wasn't subway attire.

I wasn't very far from my house when I pulled up to a red light and the car suddenly stalled. It never started again despite my desperate efforts. Horns were honking and I was feeling stressed out beyond belief, so I jumped out and flagged some passersby down. A guy came over to help me and pushed my car to the side of the road for me. I knew I'd have to get my dad to come and give me a jump to start it, but with the car safely parked at the side of the road, I figured I would continue on with my journey to Manhattan and deal with the car the next day. That meant I had to continue walking to the station. That was the easiest part of what had now become my trip into the city. I ended up taking five different modes of transportation by the time I got there. I wasn't the happiest of campers at that point. As I began each leg of the journey, I considered turning back, but I kept on. I felt a little frazzled when I finally arrived.

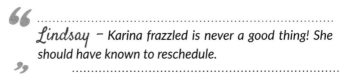

Lindsay − Karina frazzled is never a good thing! She should have known to reschedule.

The Time Warner Center wasn't there at the time, but since Columbus Circle was close to Fordham, we had decided to meet there. We were familiar with the area and knew that there were a few good places on Broadway where we could eat. When we arranged the date, I told him what I would be wearing. He told me ahead of time he would be wearing a black leather jacket. As I approached, I spotted him. This was in the late '90s, so it was one of those black Mafia-style jackets. Very East Coast looking. He looked to be two to three years older than me, and his hairline was significantly higher than it likely was originally. Whatever was left of it was brown. He was wearing trousers with a belt. He had clearly seen me right away, once I emerged from the subway, because he watched me the entire time I walked toward him.

Appearance aside, once we connected and said hello, my first thought was, *Okay, he seems nice. Sort of quiet and maybe passive.* I certainly wouldn't stop him on the street and say, "Damn, what's your name? I need to know you." He wasn't terribly hot or anything. Still, I like to take the time to get to know someone because there are often attractive qualities about a person that eventually become evident. I decided immediately since he seemed like a nice guy, I would give it some time and shake off my bad mood from my trip in, which I knew was influencing my initial lack of enthusiasm toward him, and try to enjoy the night.

He asked me where I wanted to eat. We agreed that we had to go uptown to where all the great little restaurants were, and since we were early for dinner, we decided to just walk around a bit and talk and get to know each other. Instead of talking about date-type things, likes and dislikes, he launched immediately into politics and his views on the state of our country. It was boring. I felt myself aging as we walked. Not ten minutes in, my heel got stuck in a sidewalk grate. Not stuck in such a way that I could have pulled it out. No, it was stuck, stuck. Jammed right in there and not coming out. I tried to play it cool, like I was sure I'd get it eventually, but when I gave it one good tug I broke the heel off of the shoe. As in: a clean break. The heel is probably still stuck deep into that grate.

> 66
>
> *Lindsay* – I didn't know Karina back then, but knowing her now, she would definitely take a broken heel as a
>
> 99 sign to run for the hills. I also totally understand why she stayed. Broken heels aside, she has a tendency to tough out even the most unpromising dates. Sometimes she can be a little too tough. She'll wait to see what emerges, even after a date has started to go terribly wrong. I think that's why we get along so well. I'm the yin to her yang—sometimes I'm too quick to jump overboard in the face of a bad date while she's trying to stick it out, thinking if she just gives the guy a few nips and tucks, he might wind up being her guy.

At this point, with the car and now the heel, I realized this date had gotten out of control and simply wasn't meant to be. I should have turned around right then and there and packed it in—shaken his hand and said, "Let's call it a night." But no, I didn't do that. I stuck it out. He seemed slightly worried about my ability to walk, but I kept telling this guy, "I'm fine, don't worry," as I took one step on a high heel, and then dropped down and took one on the low heel. I was alternating between being five-foot-nine then five-foot-four with each step. He called me limps-a-lot. Anyone watching would have seen me bobbing up and down, up and down, as I moved. It was crazy. He was nice enough to ask me if I wanted to go buy a new pair of shoes for the night. I didn't have enough money to do that, so I said no, that I was fine. Even if I'd had the cash, there didn't seem to be much open at that hour anyway. He suggested we take a cab, but we were so close at that point, I said no, that we should just go and sit down somewhere and eat. I didn't expect him to carry me or anything and I was trying to be a trooper, but he didn't attempt to help me walk either. He also suggested I go home and change, which obviously wasn't an option since that would have been a two-hour round-trip.

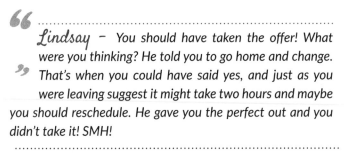

Lindsay – You should have taken the offer! What were you thinking? He told you to go home and change. That's when you could have said yes, and just as you were leaving suggest it might take two hours and maybe you should reschedule. He gave you the perfect out and you didn't take it! SMH!

As I went from tall to short and tall to short, and he kept suggesting dumb solutions to my dilemma, a lot was going through my head: A) I'm embarrassed. B) This date needs to end quickly so I can get home. I'm done with this struggle. C) This isn't going anywhere anyway because even though he's nice this guy is like, waah, waah. Blah. D) I'm livid. I should have gone home when the car stalled. E) There goes my one pair of kick-ass shoes.

Lindsay – No comment.

I put all of that out of my head and decided to give it a shot anyway. *Keep going, Karina. This is fine.* As I limped along, we found a restaurant, got a table, and took a seat. I don't remember much about what we ate, but I remember that we had drinks for about an hour and we were talking. It was all very weird—not easy or fun. Just weird. At some point, I realized my stomach was hurting—I was having cramps. I excused myself and went to the ladies' room.

Before I got into the stall to sit on the toilet, I looked in the mirror, first checking my hair and face, then spinning around a bit to check my backside and get a full look at myself. My heart basically stopped beating. I thought, *Houston, we have a problem.* Holy crap! I found myself experiencing the worst nightmare possible that a woman can have happen on a date. I wasn't wearing black, or layers, just a painted-on light-colored dress with a big stain on the back from *suddenly having my period.*

My first thought was, *Can this date get any worse?* I wanted to escape. I didn't care how much money it would have cost to get back to Staten Island. I needed to just abort the mission and escape pronto. I was going to sneak out the back door and make a run for it. I popped my head out of the bathroom to see what my options were and realized that in order to do so, I'd have to walk through the restaurant. And my date would see me. Knowing I couldn't leave, I sprung into action.

I locked the bathroom door, which by the way had a co-ed sink with a men's and women's stall. I unzipped the dress and spun it around, rationalizing that if I could wear it backward I could hold my jacket and bag in front of the stain as I walked and just get through the night. When I did that, however, there was another problem. The back was scooped lower than the front, so the top of my dress was below my boobs. Next, I took my dress off, and while standing there in my bra and underwear I put it under the water and scrubbed away at the red spot. Every once in a while someone would knock on the door and I'd unlock it and hide in the stall while they did their thing. If the person was a woman, I had to ask her to go into the men's stall to pee while I stood in my panties holding my dress in the women's stall. Between bathroom patrons, I held the dress under the hand dryer, trying to get it dry, even though it was far from clean.

About forty minutes into this fiasco, my guy knocked at the door to see if I was okay.

"I am so sorry," I said. "I'm coming out." It was a *Dumb and Dumber* moment at that point. Except, of course, I didn't use the shaving excuse. I told him I would be back out shortly. I put the dress back on only to discover that *dry-clean-only* dresses shrink from bathroom hand dryers. And the color had sort of changed—faded so it almost amplified the damage. It was a mess because you could also still see the stain. I finally wrapped my blazer around my waist, like it was a sweatshirt. The date was a mess anyway and he had to know it wasn't going anywhere. There was barely any interest on my part in making the first date happen once the heel broke, but at that point the potential for a second date was less than zero. It wasn't happening.

As I approached the table finally, looking like a disheveled mess, I realized it was likely he knew what had happened. I retraced my steps back to the table, knowing he'd most certainly checked out my ass as I walked, given where he was sitting and where I'd needed to go. He would have seen the splotch on it. My dress was so tight it would have enhanced the stain like a shining beacon. When I sat back down, he still thought it was appropriate to call me limps-a-lot. At that point, I just wanted to slap him. I was past the point of finding any humor in the situation. He was still, despite how downhill the date had gone, wanting to find out more about me. He even asked me my favorite color. Even though it's yellow, I said, "Red." We didn't discuss the period. I just told him it was time to go. Guys don't like to talk about that stuff, which was great. He had nothing to say and I wasn't going to bring it up either.

I finally got out of there that night, not one second too soon. It wasn't his fault at all. He'd done nothing wrong and was a perfectly nice guy. But with all that had happened, it was such a disaster, and I just couldn't see any point in trying again. He felt differently. He tried to call in the weeks that followed, but I pretended I had moved to another planet that didn't have phone service.

— The Over-Analyzation —

Karina

Looking back, I should have gone home when the car stalled. I'm a Capricorn and that means I'm extremely stubborn. I wasn't going to let the car take me off course. I decided to get my butt on that subway and go. The heel was different. Had that happened after the car, before I met the guy, I would have bolted. When the date ended in the worst possible way, I was reminded that we should always listen to our instincts. Nothing felt right. The date felt wrong from the beginning. I wasn't sure why, but it did. I ignored that gut feeling and that was a mistake. It took that final blow for me to realize I had had that nagging feeling about this night all along.

I never thought I'd be quoting *Pulp Fiction*, but that was definitely "divine intervention," which I should not have ignored. It reminded me of a story my grandma's friend told me a few times. The story went:

There was a very religious family living in the area that was about to get hit by one of the worst hurricanes ever. Everywhere in the media, people were urged to evacuate, but the patriarch of the family said, "Not to worry. Lord will save us. Let's pray." When the hurricane came, the rescue workers sent an ambulance to get the last of the people out. "Come with us. This is your last chance."

"Not to worry. Lord will save us. Let's pray," repeated the patriarch.

The hurricane destroyed the house, and the family was floating in the water, holding on to any floating objects they could find. The rescue teams sent in a chopper and said, "Grab the rope and we'll pull you up. This is your last chance or you'll drown."

"Not to worry. Lord will save us. Let's pray," said the dad.

Naturally, the whole family drowned and went to heaven. As they stood before the Pearly Gates, they asked God, "Why didn't you save us? We prayed to you."

The Lord answered: "Seriously? I sent you warnings, a car, a boat, and a chopper! What else could I have done?"

A few bonuses did eventually emerge from that night. Lessons, almost.

1) I have never ever left the house without something with me in case I get a surprise visit from *that time of the month*—the *Reds*, and I'm not talking about the Bolsheviks. I always plan ahead, especially when I'm wearing a practically painted-on dress. I always have something to save my butt in my possession. That was traumatic. Insanely traumatic.

2) I walk around the grates and grids on the sidewalk. I was used to a thicker heel before the incident, plus I was focused on the date. I was trying to talk and listen to what he was saying and I was walking in high heels, concentrating on foot placement and hip swaying. It was a production. It still is. So now, I have mastered looking down, swaying my hips, being cute, and not getting stuck in grates. Like, I'm an expert.

Lindsay

Karina definitely wouldn't abandon her car these days; she would probably text her date to tell him what was going on and use it as a test. If he offered to come and help her, he would have a shot with her. If he suggested a rain check, she would likely put him in check. Karina has definitely learned that sometimes the problems we encounter reveal a lot about the men we're dealing with. How a guy handles the monkey wrenches of life can be profoundly insightful. I think the most important thing for all of us to remember is to listen to our own advice. Karina, like many of us, has an uncanny ability to give some of the wisest advice I've ever heard, yet when it comes to listening to that advice, she turns the other cheek. Essentially, I think many of us have the tendency to stick something out that has disaster written all over it because deep down we have this unrelenting hope that maybe, just maybe, everything is going to turn out just like the fairy tales that we watched as little girls.

Guy's Corner

We wanted to be fair and give equal time to the guys in our lives. We know every story has two sides to it, and somewhere in the middle is the truth. Obviously, we couldn't backtrack and talk to the guys we went on these crazy dates with. Instead, we talked to three guys who know us both very well. We got the opinions of actor Ralph Macchio, who is like a big brother to Karina and me. He once joked that if Karina and I could be combined into one person, we'd be the perfect girl. Our buddy, NFL wide receiver Jacoby Jones, chimed in too—he's always got something to say about our dating life. And since most girls out there consult with their great gay friend on every dating mishap, we included ours in the discussion. The guy who listens to us and makes our hair look fabulous, celebrity hairstylist Ricardo Lauritzen.

Ralph

I do believe in signs to a point. It's a tough one. I'm not going to put too much weight personally in the signs or the universe telling her not to go. I think that sometimes around the corner might be what turns out to be the best case as opposed to surrendering because it was tough to get to that corner.

Ricardo

This date could have been seen as lucky for Karina. There are two ways of looking at it. It could have been good to see how the guy reacted in a tough situation. He had a chance to be cool and proactive about it. I would have found her new shoes, knelt down, and put them on like Karina was Cinderella.

Lindsay and Karina

As we started sharing and collecting stories from people, we found it to be contagious. We can safely say that there is no shortage of dating disasters. This next story is from a friend of a friend. She listened to the signs. Big time. We split our gut laughing about this one. Every time we think about it we laugh hysterically. And we might need to try it ourselves sometime.

The Great Escape

Giuliana, Restaurant Marketer, LA

One horrifically bad date made me do something I never would have imagined I was ever capable of doing.

I met a guy when I was working during a promotion at a restaurant. He was the bartender there, and we hit it off immediately. Although I found him to be a little bit quirky, he was amusing, and we had some good conversation that evening while we both worked.

A couple of weeks later, he invited me to join him and some friends for drinks. I met him at a bar with maybe five other people in his group. He was perfectly normal. He was clean-cut, nice, and a hard worker, trying to launch a web design business but bartending while he launched it. His friends seemed cool, which is always a good sign. He was just super sweet, and we wound up having a really great night. I had nothing negative to say after the evening ended. As we were wrapping up, he said, "I'd like to get together with you, just you and me." I agreed and thought, *Awesome, I just met someone cool.*

The night of the date arrived, and we were trying to figure out where to go. He suggested a restaurant that's not around anymore called Indochine.

Once we settled on a plan, I asked, "Do you want to meet me there or are you going to pick me up?"

"Oh no, you have to come pick me up," he said.

"Okay, I guess I can do that. Sure," I said.

"I've got some stuff going on, and I don't have transportation right now," he said.

He led me to believe that maybe his car was in the shop. So I went to pick him up. He was about twenty minutes away from where I lived. Not totally convenient, but I wasn't overly fazed by it. I felt perhaps he could have mentioned it before we started planning, but I was thinking, *whatever. it's fine.*

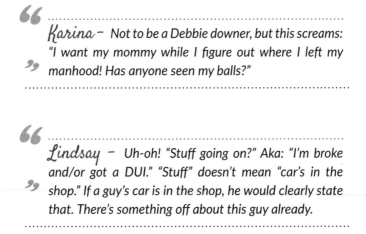

Karina – Not to be a Debbie downer, but this screams: "I want my mommy while I figure out where I left my manhood! Has anyone seen my balls?"

Lindsay – Uh-oh! "Stuff going on?" Aka: "I'm broke and/or got a DUI." "Stuff" doesn't mean "car's in the shop." If a guy's car is in the shop, he would clearly state that. There's something off about this guy already.

I pulled up and knocked on his door. He answered, but without shoes.

"Hold on," he said.

He disappeared into the back of the house and came back with a pair of combat boots that had nothing to do with his outfit. It was an odd fashion choice. I was thinking, *Okay, are we trying to go rock and roll or grungy?* Any other pair of shoes would have been a better choice with his jeans and top. I wasn't sure why he chose those shoes, but eventually his footwear decision became the least weird part of the night.

"So, is your car in the shop?" I asked.

"Oh, no," he said. "I don't have a car. I don't believe in polluting the environment in that way."

I'm thinking, *Okay. So it's okay for you to ride around in other people's cars?*

> **Karina—** Contact pollution, as I like to call it. Equally wrong. Should be saving the world with his combat boots.

Then I asked him that.

"Well, yeah," he said. "I feel a little better about that because I'm not technically the one who's contributing the pollution. I just don't want to add another vehicle out there."

> **Karina —** I think that's code for "I can't afford a car." Not to mention, unless this date happened in the '80s, these days his honorable urge to save the world could be realized in the form of a Prius.

> **Lindsay —** Pretty much, yeah.

I could not really figure out if that was actually a personal choice or if he was just full of it. I'm sure it made himself feel better about the fact that he didn't have a car.

"So, well, how do you get to work?" I asked.

"My friends drop me off or I ride my bike."

> **Karina —** Was The 40-Year-Old Virgin inspired by this guy?

"The bar where you work is like ten miles from here, in LA. You couldn't ride a bike for ten miles?"

"Yeah, well, you know, I do whatever."

At this point in the drive, I was a little suspicious, but more because I just thought he was odd. Odder than he'd revealed on drinks night. He also had a bunch of roommates, which hadn't come up and probably should have before that drive. And a few other strange things emerged. All seemed innocent enough, though. When we finally got to the restaurant, I went to valet the car.

"No, no, no, don't go valet. You don't want to spend money on valet, just go out and park," he said.

> **Lindsay** – Whoa! I don't mind self-parking but this guy is something else! I'd have ignored him and given the car to the valet!

I felt uncomfortable driving past the valet, but I did, and when I got out, I apologized to him for parking on my own. I asked him if it was okay. Since he was a nice valet guy with no attitude, he said I was fine. I told him we'd still tip him on the way out.

The discomfort of it all didn't stop there. We walked into the restaurant, which by the way was . . . how can I explain this? It was an indiscriminately Asian restaurant. It wasn't Japanese or Thai or any one specific culture but rather one of those Asian fusion restaurants. So we walked into the restaurant and he went up to the hostess stand—and he freaking bowed. As in: He put his hands together like he was doing Namaste and bowed to the hostess.

"Hello," he said. "I have a reservation for two."

She looked at him with the oddest expression on her face. She was blonde, by the way. Not Japanese. A Santa Monica blonde, blue-eyed girl. And he was bowing. Still, she took us to our table.

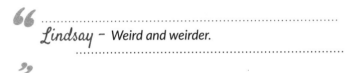

Lindsay – *Weird and weirder.*

As a side note, I'm a stickler for manners. Within seconds, his went far beyond anything I've ever seen. The hostess walked us to the table. I pulled out my chair and sat down. He, on the other hand, promptly proceeded to remove his shoes and sit cross-legged on the chair. Like he was in yoga class. I watched this happen, and then I couldn't help but comment.

"I'm sorry, why are you sitting like that? Is that more comfortable for you? Is there a reason behind this?" It was unavoidable not to discuss because it was so very strange. I was just trying to understand his thought process.

He looked at me and said, "Well, I just, I really identify with Asian cultures, so I feel more at home when I sit like this. Especially in places where the Asian culture is alive."

I thought, *what are you talking about*? I started to feel like the date was totally going sideways. He was super nice, just a little off.

The waitress came to the table, also not Asian, and he did the same thing: a quick, palms-together Namaste bow. Then we ordered drinks.

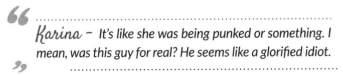

Karina – It's like she was being punked or something. I mean, was this guy for real? He seems like a glorified idiot.

It was so odd and uncomfortable. It wasn't as though we were immersed in "Asian" culture, as he put it. We weren't in Japan or even a Japanese restaurant. After we ordered our drinks, I once again couldn't help myself.

"So, what's with the bowing?" I asked, aware I might have come off as somewhat bitchy.

"I just, I really, I study a lot about Asian culture."

I knew at this point he had not said which Asian culture he was interested in and he'd used the term "Asian" a few times at that point. Two or three times already.

"So, like, I love Asian culture," he said. "I'm so very connected to them. I just find it such a beautiful way to show respect for people, especially people who are serving us."

> **Lindsay** – Serving us?!? I'd serve him a Namaste, stand up, and politely remove myself from the situation.

I took a deep breath and just sat there, hoping time would pass quickly as he sat cross-legged on his chair, absorbing the Asian-ness of this non-Asian place. My head was spinning. I thought: *Maybe you're just being a little crazy. You thought he was great before. Hang in there, the night could turn around.*

We left the Asian track when the drinks came (which couldn't have arrived soon enough), and we made small talk. I figured since he was so into Asia, he must be a world traveler. We started talking about trips and how much I loved to travel. I told him I'd traveled my entire life.

> **Karina** – I can see where this is going. I bet he's never been to Asia. Without a car and on his bike, the farthest he's gotten is probably Koreatown, at best.

So then I asked him, "Well, what about you?"

"Oh, yes. I really enjoy travel because it opens up my mind and my spirit and my heart in a way that I'm able to really accept people for who they are and not be judgmental. I'm really thankful for the experiences that I've had through travel."

My brain was twirling with curiosity about how authentic this guy was, but I asked the obvious follow-up. "Where have you traveled?"

"Well, I have a cabin in Montana that I go to really often," he said.

And then stopped.

"Anywhere else? It sounds like you really like to travel?" I asked. Due to the Namaste action and spirituality, I figured India possibly, since he had this amazing spiritual connection for anything and everything travel-related.

"I really love northern California. New York is cool too, but sometimes Manhattan really just gets to me. People are just too intense there."

In the end, it was revealed that he'd never actually left the country.

So here he was fascinated with Asia as a gross generalization, considering how many different cultures could be represented in Asian civilization.

"You seem really interested in Asia," I said, unable to help myself at this point. "Have you ever been to Asia? Are you planning on going to Asia?"

The answer was no and maybe. I was waiting for some big proclamation about him dreaming of a trip to Asia he'd been planning, but nothing. We were interrupted by the waitress taking our order and another bow on his part once it was delivered.

I realized at that point that the guy was a freak. I asked him if he studied Asian studies or anything like that, and he hadn't. He didn't even have a book he'd read that fascinated him. He didn't practice yoga. He studied web design in San Francisco. Period. I realized he was just weird and full of it and had nothing to substantiate anything he was making up to seem interesting or continental somehow. Despite my epiphany, I was a little screwed because we had already ordered. I knew the food was at least on the way, and while I waited, I spent the time dreaming up a scenario that would allow me to cut this very painful night short.

The food came and he bowed. Then he picked up his glass and toasted.

"It's so wonderful to be here with you in this moment, in this amazing place, this amazing aura. I'm just really happy to be here with you and learning about you and exploring our relationship."

I was mortified by it all. Every time he bowed, I looked down and could not make eye contact with the server, because I felt like she was wondering if I was crazy, too. After the toast, though, I just looked down at my plate and decided to dive in and get this night over with. Suddenly, before I even got food on my fork, I heard this horrendous noise coming from the other side of the table. I looked up and realized, *oh my God, he is eating like a wild animal.* He was holding the fork in his fist like a toddler learning to eat. And he was just shoveling it in his mouth. His mouth was so wide open. I could see everything rolling around in his mouth; I could even see his tonsils. He was swallowing and taking drinks each time with a noise. I had never seen anything like it. It was basically just like a wild animal sitting cross-legged in a restaurant and going to town on his Asian food.

> **Lindsay** – Check, please!

It was horrific.

Then he started peppering me with questions while he chewed: *How's your food? Try mine. Mine is good. Mine's amazing. You sure you don't want to taste it? Try it. It's so good. You've got to try this.* I obviously couldn't even consider it. I was too repulsed.

Then he stopped eating, put his elbows on the table and his chin on his hands, and said, "I'm having a really great time. Are you having a really great time? 'Cause I feel like we're connecting." Before I could answer, he stuck two of his fingers all the way into his mouth to get a piece of food out. I was close to vomiting at that point. He kept digging away as he said, "I just think you're such a great girl. You're so pretty. I'm so glad that we're out together tonight." He still had his fingers in his mouth, digging around in there for something.

> **Karina** – I'm gagging here. At this point, all I'm thinking is that I hope he believes in "finders, keepers." Sharing would be totally overrated in this case! Maybe while he's on a treasure hunt, she should hunt down the exit!

"Well, it's a little different than I thought it was going to be," I said.

"I know," he said. "I can come off as really exotic."

I decided there was no getting into any sort of normal conversation. I needed to stop talking, eat, concentrate on my food, and get out.

Suddenly, he put down his fork and, in the middle of a crowded restaurant, let out the biggest burp I'd ever heard. People turned and looked at us. It was so loud and everyone heard. I died. It was the most disgusting thing. He didn't even apologize. I looked up and he had a huge smile on his face, while I had a look of shock and horror on mine. I started to actually question my own sanity at that point, thinking, *What the hell did you see in this person the first two times you met him? Were you on drugs?*

"I'll be right back. I need to use the restroom." I grabbed my clutch and left the table to take a beat and figure out what was happening. I needed to take a minute away from this situation, because I was not only freaked out and appalled and completely disgusted by this but also had to come up with a plan as to what I was going to say when I returned to the table. I was trying to talk myself through what the next thirty-five minutes to an hour was going to look like. Instead, I just started panicking.

Inside my head while I was staring in the mirror in the bathroom, I thought: *I can't go out there. I can't. Oh God. I don't know what to do. I can't interact with this person for one more second. Maybe I can leave? Is that possible? No, I'd have to walk past him at the table and he'd see me. There's no good escape. Okay, you need an excuse. Calm down and go back and extract yourself. You can come up with an excuse. But what?*

I suddenly realized that there was one of those windows that popped out in the bathroom. And it was open. I looked at the window and thought, *Hmm, I could probably slip through that window. Should I slip through the window? What do I do?*

The fact remained: I was not spending one more second of my life with this weird guy. I could not interact with him again. So I walked to the window. I was on the first floor and the ground wasn't more than a few feet below. When I pushed the window, it opened even wider. I looked down. *I can get there.* Then before I even knew it, I was climbing out of a window. To escape a bad date. I paused, one leg in and one out. *Am I really this person? I can't. Or can I?* I had never done anything like this in my life; I have never been this person who would leave without saying good-bye. I went back and forth, thinking, *maybe I've got to do the right thing and go back.* And then I was like, *Fuck it, I'm going out the window.* So I wound up tossing my clutch out onto the pavement below then climbed out the window, which was hilarious because it happened to be right next to the valet stand. The valet parker turned around and looked at me like I was crazy. He must have watched the entire episode. I don't think he knew what was happening and, might I add, it wasn't a graceful exit in tight jeans and high heels. But I did it. Slowly, but not easily.

My feet firmly on the ground, my escape a success, I picked up my clutch, straightened my clothing, smiled at the staring valet, and started walking to my car. I handed the valet $20, apologizing as I walked by once again for not using him to park, and got in my car. Bewildered, he thanked me. I didn't even explain. I just left.

While I was driving home that night, I called multiple people immediately after to tell them that the date actually happened, because it felt surreal and I needed it on the record to be sure.

I never heard from my Asian-obsessed date again—not a text or call or anything. I was relieved.

Lindsay and Karina

She just did what many of us have only dreamed of doing but never had the guts to execute. I have to say, we give her a lot of credit. Most of us would have gone back, made an excuse, chewed the guy out, or engaged him even more just to be polite. A true escape artist—a modern-day dating Houdini!

Bad Date Blunders

I was very casually dating a few guys at one time—all the relations were in the early stages. I'm usually very good at keeping stories straight, since I juggle a lot with clients and projects all day long. My visual memory very rarely lets me down, and often I can recall every detail of my surroundings, especially when someone has told me a poignant story. The problem: Two of these new guys were named Scott and two were named Mark. Mark One told me about a fairly serious family drama. I had been intently listening and remembered every detail of the story. Quite honestly, I had thought about it after and felt badly that he was going through such a difficult time, so on what I thought was our next date, I asked him how things were going, if his dad was okay, and if everything was working out for his sister. He looked at me puzzled and said, "I don't have a sister. I'm not sure what specifically you're talking about." In my head: *OMGosh! Shoot, shoot, shoot. Wrong Mark!* It was Mark Two, not Mark One. Of course I made up some ridiculous story to cover for myself, but I was mortified. So much for dating multiple guys with the same name. Never again. Until, of course, it happened again. *—Lindsay*

. . . .

I had a first date with a guy who turned out to be super intense. And eventually revealed to me that he was a communist. He brought up the Bolshevik Revolution. Twice. That was two times too many for me. *—Sarah*

. . . .

Once I double-booked and had two dates in one night at the same time in restaurants next door to each other. I kept telling one guy I had to feed the meter every twenty minutes. I'd leave and run back to the other date. Eventually I told the other guy I had to go because the car got towed and I had to go to the pound to get it! He offered to come with me, but I kept saying, "No, no. It's fine." It was almost like the scene from *Mrs. Doubtfire*. Naturally, both guys ordered drinks, so I was pleasantly yet hastily engaging in lighthearted conversation and sipping essentially double drinks, as I frantically came up with intricate yet not obvious escape excuses. At one point, I was convinced that both men thought I had a bladder issue. I actually excused myself to use a pay phone. (No, it wasn't the '80s.) After telling the same guy a story for the second time, I realized that *double-booking* had been a terrible idea. The worst moment: I was watching one date animatedly tell me about himself, almost pleading to grab my full attention, when I went to the darkest of dark places—my mind went into a panic mode because at that point I couldn't remember who was Bob and who was Ben. The night ended when I finally said good-bye to one of the guys in front of the valet guys (who had witnessed my back and forth and gave me a well-deserved round of applause when I was finally alone). —*Karina*

. . . .

I had a second date with a tall, gorgeous, successful older man. He planned something, but he wouldn't tell me what. He just gave me a place and a time to meet him. Not knowing what to wear, I went with my fail-safe: black skinny jeans (butt looked its finest) and a cute top and heels. We met at a restaurant, but instead of going in, he said we were jumping into his car and driving to his "secret beach." He'd packed a picnic: wine, cheese, and blankets. It was incredibly romantic. We kissed under the stars as the waves crashed onto the shore. Eventually, I needed to use the restroom. I had held it as long as humanly possible. After a quick search, we decided the safest bet was behind the lifeguard stand. *Sweet relief under that moonlit sky.* Until the unthinkable occurred. My zipper broke. I worked at getting it up for five minutes, but it was hopeless. Brilliantly, I had decided to go commando that night. And my shirt was short. I had no cover. *Yay me.* I made all sorts of awkward moves to hide myself—walked behind him, held my hands strangely in my lap while executing weird poses. I even tried to distract him at one point with a: "Hey, isn't that a shooting star?" We went out again, though. He must like girls with curious body language. —*Lesley*

I had booked a facial before a date. The spa specifically told me to stay out of the sun before my session, but I had gone for a walk that morning anyway. I was appalled when it resulted in multiple small burns on my face because of the sun exposure. I tried everything from concealer to multiple foundations, but it ended up looking like I had rubbed two-day-old cake batter on my face. Needless to say, we went to a very *dark* and intimate restaurant that night. —*Natalie*

. . . .

I had been crushing on this guy for a few weeks. We'd met through friends. We had hung out in a group setting a few times, but I was hoping that he would want to hang out with me solo. He finally asked me out, but still with a friend of his who was coming down to visit. I agreed to hang out in a group setting and offered my place for them to crash, since they were coming from Orange County, a couple of hours away. The group date wasn't what I wanted, but I rallied and gathered a girlfriend to join us. We all met at a bar and proceeded to have a few drinks. Conversation was flowing, but I couldn't tell if he was into me. I was working hard-core to flirt and turn on my sarcastic charm, but I couldn't read him. I finally asked his friend, "Hey, is he into me?" To which his friend replied, "Totally into you!" So I continued to go with it. At some point, he suggested we all go to a rage at a local gay dance club. "Are you gay?" I asked. "No, I just love the music there," he said. I can't say I've ever met a straight guy so eager to go to a gay club. Still, we went and danced and drank all night and finally kissed. It was a great and perfect kiss. We went back to my place and, against my usual rules, I let him sleep in my bed but was clear there would be no sex. He agreed, but he didn't even try to cuddle. We just climbed in and went to sleep. In the morning, I almost died when I saw he was wearing rainbow pajamas. He claimed his sister made them for him and that he thought they were cute. Um. Yeah. We never spoke again. —*Malory*

. . . .

On a first date, I wore a new tank top that wound up stretching out to be a bit too large once I had worn it for awhile. It kept sort of riding down in the cleavage area, causing me to reveal a bit more of myself than I'd have liked on a first date. I had to keep tugging at it mid-conversation so it wouldn't slip down too far. I wound up dating the guy, and he told me later that he had thought that I thought he was staring at my chest too much, and that's why I was pulling up my top all the time. I guess he felt really awkward about it. He didn't tell me this until months after our first date, and he was relieved to find out the truth and that I hadn't thought he was being a dirty perv! —*Lori*

Chapter 2:
When He Knows No Limits

The Chokehold

Karina

A friend of mine had a big party at his house in Los Angeles one year on Christmas Day. There were lots of people there, but I didn't know too many of them. Most people were my age or even younger, but it was a good mix—maybe forty all together. There were a lot of attractive people and it was very lively. Almost immediately, I connected with one guy. His blue eyes were amazing, but he had the squarest shoulders. They were perfect and broad. I wasn't sure what exactly, but there was something about him that drew me in. We glanced at each other and started talking here and there. After a few conversations, I concluded he was gay. So I'd walk away, but then we'd end up chatting. I'd leave again. I found out later he was watching me like a hawk the entire time. I wasn't sure what to do because while he was nice, I kept getting the gay vibe.

Like many parties in LA, this one quickly moved into the pool. The host had tons of bathing suits and swim trunks and some people had brought them. We all changed and got in the water and then the dancing started. Since there were a few dancers at this one, we began doing some lifts and *Dirty Dancing* moves, guys lifting girls into the air. While I'd found this guy cute, and he'd made a point to partner up with me, once I swam up to him to be lifted, I decided he was definitely gay. He couldn't lift me up, mostly because he didn't quite know how to hold me. Worse, he was very awkward about it all. He kept trying and I kept falling into the water, and he would get embarrassed. It was fun, of course. But then I thought, *does he know he's gay?* I made mention of it at that point because I had to know. He stopped and looked at me and said, "I'm not gay." He laughed about it. He thought it was funny that he seemed gay to me.

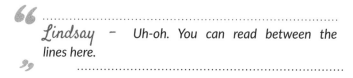

Lindsay – Uh-oh. You can read between the lines here.

We were all trying to come up with Christmas dances we could video and put up on social media. This guy seemed into it. He said, "Come on, come on, let's go dance." He was very eager. But as soon as he realized this kind of dancing involved lots of 5,6,7,8 and left side and right side, that faded. The choreography was too much for him. It was too complicated and too much information to follow on the beat. "I'll just sit this one out," he said. I let him and rejoined him later.

He quickly asked for my number, but I brushed him off initially, saying, "Let's just get to know one another first." He asked twenty more times that night. I didn't want to give in that easily. I made him work for it before I finally gave it to him.

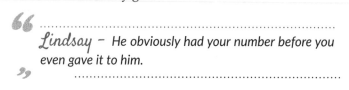

Lindsay – He obviously had your number before you even gave it to him.

For our first date, he invited me over to his place to watch a big UFC fight that was taking place. The plan was to watch the fight, then head out to have dinner after and meet up with a few friends. It was a strange plan, frankly. I felt weird going to his home first and would have much preferred to meet him out somewhere instead. But I had wanted to see the fight anyway—it was a really big one that everyone was watching—so I just went with it. I was curious to see what he had in store for the night, given the strange nature of how it was going to begin.

His Brentwood apartment was a typical bachelor pad. Not too big, clean, modern, and everything matched, so he had clearly had it decorated by someone. When he greeted me at his door, he gave me a generic hug. He patted me on the back, like you would an old relative or buddy. It was better than a handshake, but not by too much. It was one step up from a handshake. Oddly, he seemed somewhat drunk when I arrived. He was messy almost, sloppy in how he moved and spoke. Still, we sat on his big couch and got into it. The fight lived up to the hype. It was amazing. It was unclear, but one of the fighters may or may not have broken a leg. We were both excited watching it on his big screen—standing up and screaming and cheering the entire time. I was totally into it. It had a very dramatic ending right down to the last second. Though I'd been skeptical, he'd chosen a great start to the date.

Once it was over, I excused myself and went to the bathroom. When I came back out, I looked around for him. He was in his bedroom, lying half on his bed, half off of his bed, dead-to-the-world asleep. He was snoring, even. His one leg was dangling, as was one arm. It was like he didn't quite get there but fell asleep in the process. All of the lights were on and the TV was still blaring in the next room. I stared at him for a few minutes as he snored away. With the adrenaline of the fight gone, he just collapsed. I wasn't sure what to do. It was very weird. He must have been drunk before I arrived. He had passed out and wasn't getting back up.

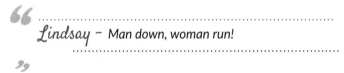

Lindsay – Man down, woman run!

After a few more minutes passed, I decided that was my cue and it was time to pack up and leave. I grabbed my things, left everything as it was—lights and TV on—and walked out, passing the doorman on the way as I exited the building.

"Leaving so soon?" he asked. "Are you guys not going to go out?"

"No," I said. "He's an amazing guy, don't get me wrong. I think he must have been tired. He fell asleep." I knew the doorman would run up and report back, so I didn't want to say that the idiot had gotten drunk and passed out on me. He nodded as I left and told me to have a good night.

I was in my car, practically home, when the phone rang. The doorman had indeed woken him up.

"Where are you? Where did you go?" He was shocked I'd left him.

"Well, you fell asleep on me. I didn't know if you were tired or drunk or what," I said. "Don't worry about it. You needed to rest, clearly."

"We were having so much fun," he said. "I don't understand why you would leave."

I thought: *Seriously?* I said again, "You fell asleep on me."

We went back and forth over that fact three or four more times. I kept saying, "Don't worry about it. It was fun. Get some sleep."

I'm not sure if it was the booze talking or what, but he was very upset about it all. I ended the call not sure what to think.

A week or so later, he started texting me again. I agreed to a second date.

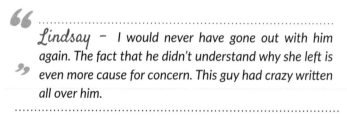

Lindsay – I would never have gone out with him again. The fact that he didn't understand why she left is even more cause for concern. This guy had crazy written all over him.

Somewhere in our broken communication back and forth, we set up a second date. When I say "we," I mean "he." He set up another date but didn't tell me. He was out and texting me, asking me where I was. I asked him what he was talking about. He said, "We have a date right now." The problem with the date: I was in Florida. He wasn't. I couldn't possibly have made the date. The trip had been planned long before I even met him. Once again, he wasn't happy. He was positive I'd agreed to the date that he was out on alone. Our second date never happened. Well, it did for him, but not for both of us together. My thought: *Wow, this guy is special.* We stopped texting each other for a while—probably a month and a half.

Then he was out somewhere and ran into someone I knew, prompting him to text me again and ask me out for a third date. The first two had been so amazing-slash-never happened, so I thought: *Why not?*

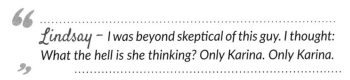

Lindsay – *I was beyond skeptical of this guy. I thought: What the hell is she thinking? Only Karina. Only Karina.*

He picked me up at home this time in a very expensive, super exotic, limited edition black matte Aston Martin. It's the car that people stop to look at and say "Wow" when it flies by. He decided to take me to a very hot restaurant—the place to see and be seen in LA at the time. It's huge and has two levels of seating, much of which faces out to the street. So, we were seen all right. As soon as that car pulled up, heads started turning to see who was going to get out of it.

I was in the passenger seat, which was close to the curb, where all the gawking people were. The place was completely full and we were parked close to the entrance and all of the packed-in people. Since it was a sports car and low to the ground, I was concerned that if I opened my door while we were too close to the curb, I'd scrape it on the sidewalk and feel like an idiot. I did not want to scratch his super duper car, especially since our previous dates had gone so swimmingly well. I thought the best thing to do was to roll down the window and stick my head out to see how close the curb was. Then I'd know how wide to open the door to slide out. What did he do? He closed the window. He didn't realize that my head was sticking out of it. It closed tightly on my neck.

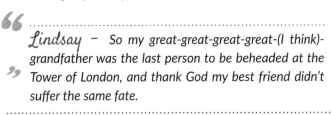

Lindsay – *So my great-great-great-great-(I think)-grandfather was the last person to be beheaded at the Tower of London, and thank God my best friend didn't suffer the same fate.*

Picture this: Crowded hot restaurant. Hoards of people staring and then yelling, "Her head is stuck! Put the window back down!" I was in pain, unable to say anything, my head hanging out the window. I could hear everyone outside of the car screaming, but I had no idea what he was doing inside the car. I was terrified. Humiliated. In pain. Embarrassed. Everyone was just watching this happen right in front of them. He was oblivious to all of it clearly, because it felt like forever before he finally figured out he needed to open the bloody window in order to release my head from the chokehold.

I pulled my head back in as soon I was able and started holding my neck, blurting out, "Oh my God! It hurts. Wow. That hurt." I actually said, "Ouweee." That was something that came out of my mouth. Then I asked, "Do you think everyone saw that?"

He looked at me and said, "Oh God. I just tried to kill you on the third date."

Once I got over the horror and humiliation of nearly being beheaded in public, we decided we would proceed with our date. We went into the restaurant anyway, even though my neck was hurting. I felt like a spotlight had followed me into the restaurant. Despite the pain, every time we made eye contact with each other during the entire meal, we burst out laughing. It was hysterical. We couldn't stop ourselves.

Whether it was technically our first, second, third, or whatever date, he didn't make a move on me. We didn't kiss until maybe the fifth or even seventh date. And that was all him. He wanted to take things slowly. That alone fed my sneaking feeling that this guy was gay and either didn't know it or didn't want to admit it. Much later, I discovered that he was indeed very, very straight.

The Over-Analyzation

Lindsay

Who gets her head caught in a window on a date? How many people can say that has happened to them? I'm guessing not many. What guy waits to kiss a girl through seven dates? Not many.

Karina

In the end—not that there weren't signs—I decided to listen to my gut instinct. That's always the best indicator. This could have landed in the dates-gone-terribly-wrong pile. But it didn't. Quite the opposite, in fact. Even though I almost got killed trying not to scratch an expensive car, it was a great date. A sign can either mean catastrophe is looming or the ride is going to be amazing. You'll know in your gut.

Guy's Corner

Ralph

Drunk on the first date is not good. He's not representing himself well enough for the long term. Her head caught in the window while checking the curb is pretty funny, and I think that he didn't do it intentionally but that probably was the straw that broke the camel's back on this guy's chances.

Ricardo

Well, I fell asleep once on a date too, so I can't really say much about that. But it shouldn't have happened with Karina. She's too interesting and always has something to say. Plus, to be drinking on the first date? He should have been on his best behavior. I didn't over-drink on a first date even in my twenties.

Lindsay and Karina

This story was just too good not to share. We heard it from a friend of a friend who heard about the book and immediately launched into this one. It's so gross. And another great reminder to the guys out there: Don't drink and date. Not in excess, anyway. You might not be lucky enough just to fall asleep on the couch. If you drink shot after shot, well, the date might not end so well.

Drank-Too-Much Guy, But Shit Happens

Elsa, Writer, Chicago

It was 1988 and I had recently graduated from college. Traveling a lot for work, I found myself in Chicago in the heat of the summer, where I contacted a friend of friends who I had met earlier in the year. We had had a "flirty connection" (as much as two twenty-two-year-olds could have in a group environment). My schedule kept me from any evening rendezvous during my trip, so the best bet for getting together turned out to be for a Cubs game on a Saturday afternoon. I was curious and figured, *Why not!?* Back then, changing a flight was a $25 proposition, so it was low risk, and the hotel on a Saturday night wasn't a deal breaker either. I was originally scheduled to leave Saturday, so it was just one extra night. I didn't know him very well, just that he was a college friend of several of my friends. Still, I extended my stay, dashed to the Gap for a pair of khakis and a T-shirt, combined these with my workout shoes and a Cubs hat, and was ready for a big day at the ballpark. Beers, beers, beers, and more beers. It was really hot and humid, so we had even more beers and a bratwurst or two. All day long.

Cubs win! The revelry in Wrigleyville sucked us in. Pizza and more beers. Barhopping here and there, thankfully via cab, as much for the air-conditioning as anything else. As we were cruising the streets and laughing, he abruptly told the cabbie, "STOP!" Out of nowhere, in the middle of nowhere. And without another word, he ran into a bar. This was not at all like the other bars we'd stopped at, so I paused before getting out. It was a rough part of town. The cabbie told me to wait—he didn't want me getting out there either. Five minutes passed. Then ten. The next thing I saw burned itself forever into the insides of my eyelids. Through the doorway of the seedy bar walked "the pooper," but I didn't know it just yet. His hands were raised, as though someone had a gun to his back. His stance was wide. He waddled toward the cab. When I rolled down the window, he sheepishly said, "Something unfortunate has happened," while slowly turning around. And then I saw it. It was as though he had sat down in deep, wet mud. Except the tops of his socks were dirty, too. That said it all. He handed me $20 through the cab window and neither of us said a word.

As the cab pulled away, I started laughing. The cabbie started laughing. And he told me, "Your friends are never gonna believe this!"

It was in the days before texts and cell phones and, thankfully for him, camera phones, so I never heard a word from him directly. But we did run into each other a couple of times over the years at weddings. Needless to say, we both have gotten a lot of mileage out of this "unfortunate" incident! Our mutual friends have yet to stop laughing.

> 66
>
> *Lindsay* – *Okay, I can say with extreme gratitude that that's never happened to me.*
>
> 99

> 66
>
> *Karina* – *Um, yeah, pretty much same here. And I hope it never does. But I guess shit happens. At least he had the courage to come out and reveal the authenticity of the downfall of the date, instead of disappearing and then later coming up with some intricate excuses: "It's not you, it's me." When it shits, Elsa, it pours. At least you can be grateful for such vivid imagery.*
>
> 99

It does remind me of another shitty story. . . .

A Gift That Keeps on Giving

A friend of mine was dating a wonderful woman. She was successful, popular, and very bubbly. They were adamant about keeping the mystery alive for as long as possible, hence they refused to ever go to the bathroom in front of each other. They never burped or farted, and there was always one night per week that was called "surprise night," meaning they would take turns planning something fun for each other as a surprise.

Well, one night he planned a very exciting evening that started off with a Broadway show, followed by a romantic dinner on the rooftop of a skyscraper with a live pianist booked just for them. Once they had dined and danced, they decided to go vodka tasting at the nearby bar. The adventure seemed innocent, since the tasting shots were very small, and they figured it would take a significant amount of them to get buzzed. How wrong they were.

An hour or so into the vodka tasting, the charming, intelligent belle started seeing double that quickly turned into triple. That was the cue for them to hail a cab and go back home. Well, by the time they arrived at their home, she was barely coherent. They made it up to their condo, and she stumbled to the bathroom in slow motion, since everything was spinning, including the porcelain throne. She grabbed it with both hands to try to land on it as centered as possible. Once the process of relieving herself was complete, she realized that getting up was an unreachable goal. "Baby!" she yelled. Baby went over to her, eager to help. As he hugged her to help her up, she whispered in his ear, "I have a surprise for you!" Intrigued and excited, he looked at her as he helped her up, just to notice that a surprise was left floating around in the throne. Next morning, he still couldn't get the image of her surprise out of his mind. So he called it "the gift that keeps on giving"!

Karina

We don't choose our family, but we do get to choose our friends. And one of our mutual friends is definitely a force to reckon with in regards to the dating scene—strong, physically and mentally, confident as only a woman in her prime can be, having her own identity in the relationship regardless of whether the man even knows he is in a relationship with her, and never submissive in an attempt to never look weak. She has a huge heart and is a true woman, undeniably and consummately sensitive.

Lindsay

I was with my son Royce, having a nice night at home, when Karina called to tell say that Melissa had met the guy she was going to marry. There was no preamble or small talk. The phone rang, and before Karina said anything else, she blurted out with certainty: "I think Melissa just met the man she's going to spend the rest of her life with." I was like, *Whoa! Melissa. The same Melissa that never likes anyone?* It was difficult not to wonder what exactly had gone on in the few hours since we'd all last spoken.

Wanna-Be-Straight Guy

Melissa, Publicist, LA

In LA, there are always a lot of so-called after-parties. Some are a blast. One night, Karina and I were on our way to Elton John's. She picked me up, and as we were driving up to the entrance of the party, getting close to the event, the streets were slightly closed off. On the little island or median in the middle stood a few sheriffs, probably waiting to stop people for a check. We were the only car around because we were really early. One of the sheriffs caught my eye; he was tall—and very good-looking. He looked like Ivan Drago from *Rocky*.

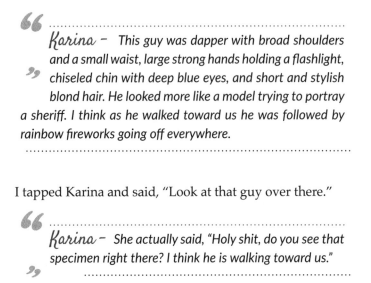

Karina – This guy was dapper with broad shoulders and a small waist, large strong hands holding a flashlight, chiseled chin with deep blue eyes, and short and stylish blond hair. He looked more like a model trying to portray a sheriff. I think as he walked toward us he was followed by rainbow fireworks going off everywhere.

I tapped Karina and said, "Look at that guy over there."

Karina – She actually said, "Holy shit, do you see that specimen right there? I think he is walking toward us."

Always the prankster, Karina pulled up beside these guys, rolled down the window, and we started messing with hot sheriff guy. Once we started talking to him, we realized he was taller than I'd thought originally—maybe six foot six inches. He was more handsome close-up, too. And a dude. Manly looking. We started joking with him through the window, so he walked over, leaned down, and began talking to us. We were having a blast. For me, it was 100 percent joking, because I was with Karina—and in my mind, with every guy, they always choose Karina. She is stunning and guys are immediately drawn to her. So I was busting on this guy, never thinking he'd be remotely interested in me. I'm used to that with her and it's cool. It was not insecurity. She's just beautiful. It turned out, like Karina and Drago, this guy was Russian. So it was kind of funny.

After a few minutes, he said, "Let me give you my card. It has my number." He pulled out two of them and started to hand one to each of us.

Karina – My recollection is a bit different: After about ten minutes of small talk with our tall, exquisite ball of testosterone leaning into the window on the driver's seat, *he pulled out a card with his number, and without making any eye contact with me or Melissa, said, "I would love to give you my number if that's okay." He looked straight at Melissa and handed her the card, and without even glancing at me or in my direction added, "Sorry."*

....

"Oh, no, no, no," I said, stopping him. "You can't give us both your number. We can't do that. You're going to have to give it to only one of us. You'll have to choose."

I was totally joking to see what he would do. So he looked at Karina and he looked at me. He pulled out a card and turned to Karina and said, "I'm so sorry, but I'm going to have to give it to your friend."

Karina thought it was the best thing since sliced bread. She was so excited for me. She was shocked. I was dying of laughter. The whole thing was just funny and fun.

66 ....

Karina – *I saw the way he looked at her. It was the way a man looks at a woman he's very interested in. He had a sparkle in his eyes that coyly undressed Melissa in his mind. He meant business (especially with a gun and a pair of handcuffs hanging off his belt) and he was going after what he thought he wanted. Melissa was beaming, and understandably so, and I was ecstatic and calling Lindsay to say we needed to plan a wedding! Sure, I might have moved too quickly, but if you were there and experienced the fireworks, you probably would have done the same. Frankly, that's the only time in the ten years I have known Melissa that I saw her get so excited and giggly over a man. And who could blame her? He was a young, sexy, vibrant version of Dolph Lundgren! I wasn't going on a date with Dolph, but I was there in spirit and filled with the same girl-like excitement that Melissa's*

Prince Charming had arrived in a sheriff's uniform and with a halo around him.

....

We pulled away and went into our event. The entire night, I was so excited. We were doing the total girl thing, with Karina insisting I was going to marry this guy, and I was trying to relax but was pretty much wound up about it. Armed with his number, I waited about thirty minutes and texted from the event, making certain he had my number. He texted me right back. We went back and forth on text for another twenty minutes, and he seemed sweet. He wasn't aggressive, but he was charming. He told me I was beautiful and said all sorts of nice things a woman likes to hear. He was playing his cards perfectly. Eventually, he texted that he wanted me to enjoy my time at the event and to call him or text him when I was finished.

Karina and I hung out at the event for a bit and then decided to hit the road. I said to Karina, "Whatever you do, take a different way out. I don't want to drive by him again. That would be weird. It's too much. I don't want to talk any more tonight."

And what does she do? She drove down the same street and she stopped right in front of him. She rolled down the window and she started messing with him and said, "I think this is a great match."

I almost died, but he leaned down to my window and we talked for a bit. He was super nice and flirty. Karina was jumping in and embarrassing me completely, but it was funny. We eventually pulled away, but he and I were texting back and forth until four that morning. He was on duty, so he couldn't call. But I was totally impressed by him and bewildered as to why this guy was still single.

The texts got strangely intense quickly.

Sheriff: Do you want marriage and kids?

Me: Yeah. Really. Do you want marriage and kids?

Sheriff: I would love marriage and kids, but I don't know if I could. I have a secret.

Me: Well, are you going to tell me?

Sheriff: If I tell you, I'm just going to scare you off, and I don't want to scare you off because I'm really interested in you.

Me: If you don't tell me now, then you're going to scare me off either way. So it's either you tell me or you don't.

Sheriff: OK, I'm going to tell you because I respect you, and I don't want you to get freaked out. I really want you to give me a chance, even if I'm going to tell you this.

Me: OK.

Sheriff: I've not always been with women.

Me: So you're bisexual, or are you gay?

Sheriff: Well, I'm bi.

Then we had an entire conversation about being bisexual.

> 66 ....
> *Lindsay* – When I first heard about this interesting text exchange, I was certain: He's gay. He's totally gay. 99 He's not bisexual. You don't bring that up on the first night just texting. But in that moment, I think he wanted everyone including himself and Melissa to believe he was straight. He must have thought that he could have a beard, but that rarely works out now, does it?
> ....

> 66 ....
> *Karina* – He simply hadn't found the right woman. That was it. He was straight.
> 99 ....

> 66 ....
> *Lindsay* – Delusional. Karina is delusional!
> ....
> 99

Karina − As an eternal optimist, especially when it comes to love (as it pertains to others especially), I thought that maybe, just maybe, being the sheriff in West Hollywood, the gay capital of Southern California, he was just a little confused. And since he said he wasn't gay, there was a chance this could work. I don't give up easily. Just because he had a very "light" history dating women, and liked to double dip, and possibly had more "dick pics" on his phone than existed on the World Wide Web, there were still perks that could have come from this relationship. He would be super fashionable and wouldn't be shy to share his opinion on appearance, he would be an amazing shopping buddy, and gay men make amazing best friends! Okay, okay, all jokes aside: How dare he waste Melissa's time? As a member of the police force, he should be arrested and manhandled—wait . . . he might have liked that. Well, if he needed a beard, he should have just grown one!

I didn't get too carried away with him over the next couple of weeks. We spoke a lot and had conversations about being gay versus bisexual, but I made an effort to not let myself get involved with him beyond that. He tried every day for those two weeks to take me out, insisting he really liked me and pleading with me to give him a shot. He wanted to be with women only. He didn't want to be with guys anymore. I knew this wasn't a great situation for me, but I also wished he were straight. We really enjoyed talking with each other and definitely clicked. It was difficult to keep my distance, and at the end of the day, I felt certain there was a reason he came into my life. I remained hopeful in some small way, but mostly I felt this guy was lost, and for that I felt awful because he was so nice. I have so many friends and I didn't have time to save the world, but for this guy, I felt I needed to make time.

Whatever my intentions at the time, a week later, I agreed to go out with him, surprising myself. My gut instinct is usually dead-on with guys, but in this case, I wasn't sure what was happening. I was drawn to him; that was for certain.

66 ....

Lindsay – Had Melissa been in her right mind and listening to what he was actually saying on their calls, I would have been okay with her going out with him as friends. However, she kept telling me about their discussions, which made it crystal clear to me that he was gay and trying to convince himself that he was bisexual. She would tell me things he would say, like, "I think I'm bi. I mean, I've been with a lot of women." At which point I told her to ask him if he had been with more men than women or women than men, to which he responded "men"—that out of hundreds of lovers only two had been women. I thought, How much more obvious does he need to get? This guy was clearly gay.

....

I decided to meet him for coffee with his sheriff partner. I was just in a different place. He was so good with words and he was very endearing. The three of us chatted over coffee.

He and I met one more time about a week after that. I learned that no one knew he was gay. He came clean with me; he was gay. But he'd never told anyone at work—or his family. He admitted he was struggling with his identity and didn't know how to handle it, but through talking with me, he realized he was totally and completely gay.

Two funny things came of all of this: First, Hot Sheriff and I became friends. We still talk sometimes. And I set him up with one of my gay friends. There was a reason he came into my life and, looking back, as confusing and weird as it was, I'm glad he did. Second, his partner wound up asking me for my number. He liked me. We did some back and forth, but he wasn't aggressive enough so it didn't really go anywhere.

> **66** ....
>
> *Lindsay* – *He would have to be really aggressive to handle a woman like Melissa. She plays softball and flag football.*
>
> **99**
> ....

The moral of the story is that you can't ever change someone. Sometimes we think we can, but we cannot change a guy's stripes. Hot Sheriff fit the bill initially more than any guy I've ever dated. He was great upfront—he gave me the appropriate amount of attention and communicated well. But he was gay. He would have made a great boyfriend.

> **66** ....
>
> *Lindsay* – *A great boyfriend??? Umm, okay. Melissa fell into the trap that we all do at some point or another, when a good-looking guy makes us feel great about ourselves and on paper looks amazing. Once we realize something is off, we have already gotten to know him in our imaginations, despite knowing very little about him—if anything at all. I could see how excited she was about the "idea" of him before she ever even knew which way he was swinging.*
>
> **99**
> ....

> **66** ....
>
> *Karina* – *Well, okay, so he was gay. I can totally sympathize with a person going through hell emotionally trying to figure out his sexuality, but with all that said and done, putting a woman in the middle of a personal struggle is not fair. If you are not sure then take your time to figure it out, but there is no need or given right that it should be done at someone else's expense. As for our sheriff, even though I think he played us both, at least he had the dignity and respect to let Melissa know the real situation before things got too far and hearts were broken.*
>
> **99**
> ....

Lindsay and Karina

Lisa Ann is a perfect storyteller, and boy does she have great stories. We remember hearing this one for the first time and thinking: *Wow, we have nothing on Lisa Ann.* We think this one is in the top ten dating stories.

Can I Wear Your Dress?

Lisa Ann Walter, Actress, Writer, Comedian, LA

It was spring break, in the '80s when I was in college, and I was drinking a lot. I was staying down in the Fort Lauderdale area with a friend of mine from high school who had moved there. We went out every night—as I said, we were on spring break. In fact, on the trip down there—this is really interesting—I was in the backseat with an actor. We went to school together, and we made out the entire way in the car down to Florida. Literally, we tongue-wrestled for a thirteen-hour trip. And when we arrived, we went out and we were partying. I wish I had just stuck with the guy in the back seat. I met a guy at a dance club, and I was wearing a leopard print dress and black spike heels. Very New Wave. I thought I looked very cute. Come on, it was the '80s! I met this guy who looked like—I can see his face to this day—absolutely the most stunning man I've ever gone out with. Like an angel. Like Brad Pitt. A young Brad Pitt. Gorgeous. Like Brad Pitt in *Thelma and Louise*. So anyhow, he was a little shorter than I like in a guy—maybe 5'6"—but very muscular, sinewy. He was so gorgeous and a little bold; he came up to me and complimented my dress and kept complimenting me. And I thought, *Oh, wow.* He danced with me, and at the end of the night, he asked, "Can I take you to breakfast?" And I said, "Sure." He'd been feeding me drinks all night, and I felt a little woozy. So we went out, we laughed, and we talked.

We wound up, long story short, back at my friend's place, making out. Then he asked me a question that I'd never heard on a date before and I've never heard since. He again complimented my dress and my shoes . . . and then he asked if he could wear them.

And he wasn't kidding.

First I said, "Oh, ha ha, you probably couldn't fit into them . . ." and he said, "No, I'd love to—I want to try them on." Now, I wasn't completely sheltered because I grew up in a major city. But, it turns out, this guy did not. He came from a dry town in the middle of, I don't know, Bum Fuck, Georgia, somewhere. And he was really sheltered. And busting out of there to go on spring break in Fort Lauderdale was the first time in his life that he got to let his freak flag fly.

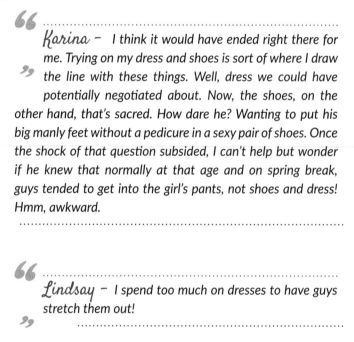

Karina – I think it would have ended right there for me. Trying on my dress and shoes is sort of where I draw the line with these things. Well, dress we could have potentially negotiated about. Now, the shoes, on the other hand, that's sacred. How dare he? Wanting to put his big manly feet without a pedicure in a sexy pair of shoes. Once the shock of that question subsided, I can't help but wonder if he knew that normally at that age and on spring break, guys tended to get into the girl's pants, not shoes and dress! Hmm, awkward.

Lindsay – I spend too much on dresses to have guys stretch them out!

Well, it did *not* happen, but wait . . . the story's not finished! I still made out with him and we were seriously going at it. I mean, I was drunk; he was gorgeous. He took my hand and started to put it down into his pants, but first he warned me that he had a little issue. And *little* issue is exactly what was going on down there. We're talking about two inches. We're talking—I don't know what the politically correct term is these days—a hermaphrodite. Maybe now we call it "non–gender specific." Back then we just had "hermaphrodite." I wasn't sure what was happening. I never want to hurt anyone's feelings. I really don't. The poor guy. How much action could this guy have gotten in his tiny little town in Georgia? He was probably afraid to ever do anything. And so he said, "Don't worry about me," and he dove down south on me. Well, after a minute, I just yanked him up by his hair and said, "Honey, don't worry. With a tongue like that, you don't need a penis." And no kidding, to this day it's probably the best oral sex I've ever had. Later, with hindsight, I figured it was because he had to know what to do. He would have figured it out based on his situation.

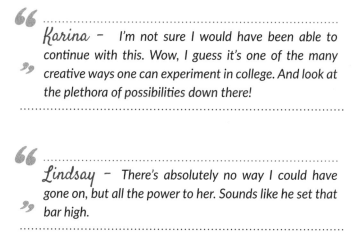

Karina – I'm not sure I would have been able to continue with this. Wow, I guess it's one of the many creative ways one can experiment in college. And look at the plethora of possibilities down there!

Lindsay – There's absolutely no way I could have gone on, but all the power to her. Sounds like he set that bar high.

Let me reiterate: I was drunk; he was gorgeous. Honestly, though, he was so pretty and so charming and delightful for the entire night up to that point that it kind of took me too long to figure out that he wasn't kidding about wanting to wear my clothes. Once he figured out that I wasn't going to go for it, he just dove back into kissing me. And I was just drunk enough to keep going. You know, there are some things that happen in your life that make you go, *Hmm, maybe I shouldn't drink quite so much.* That was one of them.

If anyone asked me today if he could wear my shoes, it would be a deal breaker. I've already had the first husband tell me that he was into dudes as well—but that's a story for your next book!

Best Worst Pickup Lines Ever

(Yes! These really happened.)

Are you religious? Because you're the answer to all my prayers.

. . . .

I'm not a photographer, but I can picture you and me together.

. . . .

Did you sit in a pile of sugar? Because you have a pretty sweet ass.

. . . .

I seem to have lost my number, can I have yours?

. . . .

Do you live in a cornfield? Because I'm stalking you.

. . . .

My buddies bet me that I wouldn't be able to start a conversation with the most beautiful girl in the bar. Wanna buy some drinks with their money?

. . . .

Do you have a map? I'm getting lost in your eyes.

. . . .

Do you know what my T-shirt is made of? Boyfriend material.

. . . .

If God made anything more beautiful than you, I'm sure he'd keep it for himself.

. . . .

Chapter 3:
I'm Not Banging You Just Because...

Pervy I-Won't-Sleep-With-You-Just-Because-You're-A-Pro-Athlete Guy

Lindsay

Uh, I'm just not into *that*.

Karina had just announced she was engaged again. For this one, we decided to book a night at the Venetian and went to sit by the pool. It was a typical Vegas day: hot, sunny, and the pool crowded with partiers looking for fun in the sun. No one interested me all too much. Mostly Karina and I were just hanging with friends and getting some sun. But, almost immediately, I noticed a really hot guy in the cabana next to us. Without even thinking about it, we started making eye contact. Smiling, flirting, whatever—I couldn't help myself. He was cute. Light-skinned black, short short hair, but super long and lean. Handsome. I realized right away who he was since I love NBA basketball. And he was playing right along. We didn't chat, but we didn't need to. We said a quick "hello."

> ❝
>
> *Karina* – Sometimes I wonder if I'm just a hopeless romantic who's willing to do whatever it takes to make it work, until I come to the point that sometimes that's just not enough. Then after feeling sorry for myself, I turn on The Bachelor or Bachelorette and find myself thinking that actually, in most of the cases, I just got off easy. Not to mention, it's not about how many times you try but about getting to that magical place of being in love and being loved once. Anyway, enough about math and let's get back to the very handsome, tall man who was wooing my best friend with his charm . . . and smile . . . and swagger . . . and attention, while being surrounded by a group of very attractive, half

naked, very willing female participants. Even though he didn't lack attention, the "star" made a point of coming over to us to chat and have drinks. Needless to say, Lindsay definitely liked it, and so did I. And who wouldn't? Attention is a very delicious and desirable drug.

That night, we got all decked out in our strappy sparkly dresses and heels and hit Tao nightclub. The music was loud, the crowd was pumped, and the tequila was flowing; we were having a great time. Our hostess had strategically placed us within eyeshot of my pool guy's table. Sure enough, within half an hour I spotted him again coming in with a crowd of his own. And he was seated right there at the table next to us in the VIP section. Professional basketball player guy and his entourage and me. Even in the dark, with just lasers and glimmers of light, and with all of his clothes on, I could see that he was really, really attractive. Hot. He was also there celebrating something, but we weren't sure what. We could tell by the little toast someone gave before they started drinking. We were all in a roped-off section. I didn't really spend much time taking notice of him; instead he came over and started chatting me up. He was actually quite sweet and very charming. When I looked around, I realized I was the envy of a lot of really thirsty girls (aka groupies). It was funny to watch all of these girls wagging their tails on the other side of the club trying to connect with him or make eye contact. It was hilarious and entertaining.

Karina had seen what was happening and so she got up and asked to take a photo with all of us. Everyone got up for the shot, and then when we sat back down, he quickly laid on the charm. Within seconds it was confirmed that he was easy on the eyes, super sexy, and just fun to be around. I fell right for it, and the two of us spent the night dancing up a storm. We were up above the crowd, sectioned off, dancing on some sort of banquette. The funny thing was, the little groupies were giving me the dirtiest looks and were clearly furious that I was dancing with this guy all night, holding all of his attention. They were staring me down. They were totally jealous. They wanted to eat me alive. He even said, "Those bitches would take you out if they could." We laughed about them the entire time we were dancing. He pointed out one girl who followed him everywhere he went, city to city. She was long on cleavage, with an unrelenting stare—dagger-filled—right at me. Her dress was too tight and too high, and her look was so icy it was as though I was dancing with her boyfriend.

Not that I couldn't appreciate her interest, but she was definitely on the other side of obsession. He was charismatic, tall, and handsome, and all eyes were on us. He was whispering in my ear a lot, talking about how he'd like to see me sometime in another city when we were both in the same place. He was sweet, and every once in a while, he'd kiss my neck or pull me in for a hug. It was fun and I really liked him, but I knew exactly what to expect with pro athletes.

We spent the entire evening together well into the early morning. At around what felt like three or four in the morning, we were all ready to pack it in. I assumed he'd ask for my phone number and that maybe I'd see him again sometime, somewhere.

> *Karina* − *Umm, I'm sure deep down somewhere he wanted to see if Lindsay would meet up with him for dinner to discuss the current state of our nation's affairs or maybe even the best literature has to offer. In reality, a stereotypical perception of athletes is slightly different. But with his looks, flowing tequila, and plenty of "cutthroat" bitches watching us, it was a night to remember.*

Before we got to that, just as I went to grab my stuff, all of a sudden, he said to me, "Come back and spend the night with me." I'm not going to lie, a part of me was intrigued, but another part (the smarter part) knew that this was his MO. Charming and laying it on thick. I knew that I wasn't special. This was likely a regular thing with him. I stood there for a minute dazed, thinking, *huh?* It was uncomfortable. He must have known by the look in my eye that it wasn't happening. He even said "please" to make an extra push. "I want to get to know you." I thought: *Yeah, get to know me? I'm sure you would.* I declined the offer.

I wasn't one of the groupies, who, by the way, we'd made fun of all night while we danced—laughing at how they were so angry and so desperate to be around him. I wasn't even thinking that's how this was going to play out when we were dancing. Absolutely not. I was disappointed because I thought he was a super nice, well-spoken, talented, fun guy. We had had such a good time. He wasn't all over me in any disrespectful way. He occasionally softly kissed me, but in a very sweet and not overly aggressive way, like a lot of guys that I'd met or gotten involved with usually had. I was quite interested up until the very end of the night.

After I politely declined, he tried to tell me that he would see me at his room. After I had declined the offer, it became less of an invite or anything I apparently had any choice in. It was a directive. Like who wouldn't want to be told to go sleep with him? It was such a waste of such a beautiful specimen.

Still, I said, "Okay. That sounds great. What's the room number?" He told me and then I said, "See you there. I just have to get Karina to her room, then I'll be there."

We let them leave the club first and then we hustled out of there. Of course, I never showed up. I dropped Karina at her room and went straight to mine. I told him I'd be there and then didn't show. Anything else just wasn't my style.

The Over-Analyzation

Lindsay

It's not like I thought I'd met Mr. Right. Not at all. And it's not like someday I wouldn't have wanted to see him again. I'm not naïve—he wasn't seeking my hand in marriage. I work in the business and I know about athletes and how they are the majority of the time. I was simply surprised that he would expect me to sleep with him, especially after getting to know me a little bit—that he would think that I was that type of girl. As I got ready to go to bed—alone in my own room—I at least got a laugh at the thought of him sitting or lying there waiting for me to spring through the door ready for action. I wonder how long he waited before he figured out I was a total no-show. I always hoped I'd run into him so I could ask.

Karina

He probably thought you made him work for it. It's simple supply and demand. The more supply of willing girls there are, the less they are in demand. Lindsay played her cards right. There are also quality guys, and he just wasn't one of them. It's an interesting aspect of dating: You meet a guy and you have instant connection and chemistry. Naturally, as a woman you will instinctively start flirting with him, showing your interest in him. He, on the other hand, might take that to mean you are interested in not just getting to know him but getting to know his package right off the bat. He gets confused about crossing that line. And sometimes doesn't even know a line exists. You can only show interest and put your best foot forward, and if he doesn't recognize quality, well, then that's just on him.

Guy's Corner

Jacoby

First, I think she went up to his room. I'm joking. Lindsay is a good-looking girl. What guy wouldn't go for it? Some girls might have been okay with that. But Lindsay was totally right not to go. Though, I think she did.

Ralph

I've been with both Karina and Lindsay. When they walk in a room, they have a wow factor. I've watched and witnessed arguably intelligent men become bumbling idiots around them. I've walked into a room and been the center of attention, but I have never rendered anyone speechless. Still, even if he was that into Lindsay, I think certainly there was a classier approach. Then again, if you're a celebrity, you have that spotlight, and maybe that becomes the norm for them in the dating scene or the one-night-stand scene. Lindsay was right to not go.

Ricardo

Really? They were at a club in Vegas? That's so not like them. Seriously, though, Lindsay has something that I find to be very magical and I wish I had a little bit of it myself. She does not give herself to anybody who doesn't have value, an importance, or who doesn't bring something special into her life. She did the right thing.

The A-List Non-Talker

Karina

A-list star doesn't necessarily mean A-list date. Lindsay and I had taken a trip to Hawaii, and on the flight back, she turned and pointed out that a fairly famous and talented actor was sitting nearby. I couldn't turn around to see him without being obvious, so instead I decided to make a quick trip to the bathroom. I stood up to see where this guy was and bam—suddenly we were face-to-face. I'd more than spotted him. He'd stood up at the same time and there we were in the aisle of the plane with our faces five inches apart from each other.

"Well, hello," I said.

He smiled, and after a short but lively conversation, he asked for my number.

We texted a lot for the next couple of weeks while he was away shooting a film, getting to know each other, until finally he suggested we meet up. His texts had been fun and articulate. They led me to believe he was a great guy and interesting, since we'd texted about art and other common interests. He seemed pretty amazing—if texting was a measure. I agreed to meet him and said I thought it was best if we met somewhere quiet, away from the paparazzi, so that we could actually relax and concentrate on talking, rather than working on how not to get photographed. That way we could better enjoy each other's company.

His pick for our date: a bar in a hotel where people go to be seen. The one place where there are always paparazzi camped out. Not only did he pick a populated, not-private hot spot, as the hostess was walking us in to be seated, he suggested the most front-and-center table facing Rodeo Drive. It couldn't have been any less private or discreet. It was an odd choice, but I went with it. It turned out to be the least odd thing about the date.

We sat across from each other, at first in somewhat of an awkward silence. Even though I didn't take him for a shy guy, I thought that once we ordered drinks, he would warm up and we would be chatting away. The waiter definitely took his time to take our order. While we waited, we tried small talk but it wasn't catching on. I asked him about his family, work, hobbies, love or hate of sports, anything and everything I could think of, and for the most part I got extremely long answers, which wasn't bad at all. It's just they were being delivered at such a slow speed that by the time he would get to the middle of the sentence, I was struggling to remember the beginning of it. It was early in the evening, but by the time the waiter came to take our order, I knew I had to order a double to get through this. I was trying to have a normal conversation, but unlike on the plane or even through texting, this time he was talking abnormally slow. So slowly, that at one point I thought I heard a dial-up tone as he was thinking of the next word. I'm not exaggerating, either. It was like he was speaking in slow motion. It was so bad, I started playing games in my head to see if I could finish the sentence for him or guess what he was going to say. And it wasn't just the pacing of his words. He didn't have a lot to say.

66

Lindsay – Maybe he had spent some time with Tommy Chong earlier in the evening?

99

I tried to come up with topics, but it was almost like I was talking to a wall. I started going through all of my classes in college—art, politics, even statistics. That one did get a little zing out of him. He seemed to like talking about statistics for whatever reason. My college course load exhausted, I eventually looked out the window, grasping to find a subject matter that might be good to talk about for us both. He followed my gaze, looked outside, and then said, "Aren't . . . palm . . . trees . . . amazing?"

Palm trees? The trees outside? "Uh, yeah—I don't know. What do you mean?" I asked.

"Yeah. (Long pause.) Well (longer pause), they're skinny (long pause). And . . . so . . . tall. And they don't fall."

Oh my God, I need another double.

66

Lindsay − All I see in my mind is Karina looking like a bobblehead doll with her polite smile, her wide eyes, and that head nodding as though on a coiled spring.

99

The chemistry didn't appear to be there. Still, we had one drink, shared an appetizer, and believe it or not, remained seated there until 10:30 or so—three-plus hours. I scrambled to figure out new topics of discussion, while he said a few words per minute. It was the strangest thing ever. As we were leaving, he asked me to go for Mexican food at a place he loved.

"Is it close by?" I asked.

"Yeah," he said. "Ten minutes away. Follow me in your car."

We ended up driving forty minutes away. I followed him there, but by the time we got there, the restaurant was closed. I was actually relieved. This was just not a good date. It wasn't working. He pleaded with the place to serve us at least a margarita, since we'd driven all the way there.

I wanted out, but I was stuck, because they agreed to serve us. I literally inhaled the drink and then said, "Oh look, we're done. I guess it's time to go."

He walked me to my car.

"It was a pleasure meeting you," I said. "I think we can both agree that this isn't for us."

I don't actually know if he agreed or not because he just stood there trying to smile. He may have thought it was good because he might not have been aware of how difficult he was to talk to that night. In my opinion, he definitely crashed. But yet again, he might have thought *I* talked too much. There was no telling with him. Still, I suggested that it would be best if we didn't share this with anyone. Tabloids love juicy stories, and even though this one was far away from juicy, if we could have just kept the night between us that would have been great. We didn't need to make a big thing of it. He seemed to agree with me and we parted ways after a hug.

The next day I woke up to the story all over the tabloids that he and I had gone on multiple dates and were in fact an item.

> 66
> ....
> *Lindsay* – Shocker. You and A-lister sit in plain view at a notorious celebrity hotel and hope that it doesn't get picked up in the media? I warned you.
> ....

We avoided each other after that. My publicist has told me that a couple of times at events we've come close to interacting, but she always works to make sure we'll miss each other by a minute. And every time I see a palm tree I think, *Wow, that's actually quite amazing.*

— The Over-Analyzation —

Lindsay

I actually love this date because it had so much potential, yet when it went wrong, Karina didn't try to heroically salvage it. She took it for what it was and learned something new about the awesomeness of LA palm trees. But seriously, I love that she didn't try to turn this toad into a prince and never looked back.

Guy's Corner

Jacoby

All he did was talk about palm trees? Whether or not you're with an A, B, C, D, E, F, whatever lister you want to be, I figure they're about the same. But I think you still have to treat Karina with some respect and also have some for yourself. Palm trees? She probably has not saved this guy's number.

Ricardo

A-listers aren't great dates. They only talk and focus on themselves. The entitlement is real. They think they don't need to do anything even sexually; they can just lay there and let you do all the business. Palm trees?

Lindsay and Karina

This story has movie scene written all over it. It reminds me of a scene in *There's Something About Mary*. The cool agent and his misfiring pistol. There was no way we were going to write a book about misadventures in dating and not include this story. I think this one really scarred Lily.

Johnny-Come-Lately, Err, Quickly

Lily, Producer, LA

For weeks after meeting this guy, a former CAA agent who left to go elsewhere, we would talk on the phone and text. He was traveling so much that we weren't able to make a time to meet, but we had a great time on the phone and the time passed quickly. He was really funny, and it was sort of nice to be courted a bit ahead of connecting in person. I was impressed because so few guys actually call these days. He called and he was sweet.

I'm always nervous about dating people I don't know too well, so I did my research on this guy and he totally checked out. He was legit. I agreed to meet him for coffee, and eventually, after a great time and great conversation, he offered to make me lunch at his place. I agreed, feeling comfortable enough about him at that point to go to his place. He told me he loved to cook. I thought it was cute.

After we picked up groceries, we went back to his place. We were going up in the elevator, and at one point he pushed me back up against the wall and started making out with me. It was a good kiss, but it was certainly a little more intense and happened much sooner than I expected. But I thought, *I can slow it down inside.* We reached his floor and walked to his apartment. Keep in mind, this was a successful and accomplished professional in his thirties. His house was like a frat house at best—like something a twenty-one-year-old right out of college or even still in college would live in. There were broken vertical blinds, hanging off the rail. It was a disaster. It was sparse and messy. Not clean, not well decorated. I knew his car was nice, as I'd seen it. I knew he traveled the world and represented super celeb clients. But his house was a shit hole that he didn't take care of at all.

I ignored the weirdness of the situation and the fact that his home life didn't match at all the persona he lived publicly. Still, I hung out with him in the kitchen while he made lunch, and eventually we sat in his weirdly empty living room—on the couch in front of the TV. The only two things in the room. We started kissing again. He was sort of aggressive, but I tried to lead his hands away when he got too much so. I wasn't being a prude. At one point, for less than a minute, I had my hand on his package. He had his pants on and fully zipped. It was all very teenager-ish. Nothing X-rated. Just making out on a couch. I moved my hand and told him I wasn't ready to move so quickly, like a teenager. Without warning, with his pants on, he came. Bam. Out of nowhere. I can't even stress how much I barely touched it. He had to get up and go get a towel and change. He'd soaked himself. It was obvious he was uncomfortable about what had happened.

" ....

Karina – *Oh dear. Poor thing. I guess self-restraint was something very foreign to him. We all know what a "quickie" is, but this must have been the quickie of all quickies. He might have had superior endurance in business, but in the bedroom department I think it's safe to assume that he had mastered premature ejaculation. On the bright side, there was no unprotected sex, since a couple of layers of clothing provided enough shield not to have postmortem worries. Misfire had definitely backfired!*

....

When he came back to the living room, he said, "I need to go to the Nike store." That was it. The most out-of-left-field thing, but probably all that he could think of in his embarrassment.

I'm obviously not a guy, but in my experience at that age, by that point in time, it shouldn't be such a surprise that you're about to come. It was so confusing for me. I wasn't sure if he really had no clue what was happening or if that was his intention all along. He was thirty-eight. Did he just want to quickly bang one out like that or was it a total misfire?

I left. He tried to feebly stay in contact, checking in to see if I'd landed a consulting gig I had bid on and texting a bit here and there. But I couldn't get back into it with him. It had been just a little too strange for me. He was great on the outside, but once I saw what was going on in his home and then "the incident," well, the romance died on that couch.

Karina and Lindsay's Rules to Date By

1. Trust your women's intuition. It's usually right.

2. Don't mistake cruelty for sarcasm. It will only get worse.

3. Don't trust a man who spends more time than you in front of the mirror. It's a relationship, not a competition.

4. Compliments: Learn how to give, take, and keep them coming. Men love being rewarded for good behavior.

5. Never sacrifice anything, especially if you are asked to do so. Compromise is fine, but it's a two-way street. He needs to compromise as well.

6. Go after your dreams and goals instead of waiting for your Mr. Right to validate your existence. He'll respect you and value you that much more for doing so.

7. If a man you are with doesn't give you wings to fly, but rather ties anchors to your ankles, it's time to go! Cut him loose.

8. If the person stimulates you, you are a legend in your own bed. And if not, it's the definition of the eternity. When he comes, she goes. . .

9. "Everyone has baggage. Just make sure his is carry-on."

10. He had his shit and I had my shit, and together it created a whole bunch of shit.

11. Don't look for a sugar daddy. Be your own sugar mama!

Chapter 4:
The Tight Wad aka Cheap Ass

Sex Tape Gone Wrong

Karina

When things get passionate quickly, sometimes we don't use our best judgment. I met a uniquely handsome guy at an Emmy party once—not model handsome, but he had a spark in his eye that was mischievous and he had charisma. He was dark with piercing blue eyes. Usually I don't go for guys who have that chiseled look because I like men with a brain too, but he was tall and muscular and really handsome. He was shy but also funny. There was just something about him. Like 99 percent of the people in LA, he was an actor. He was waiting for his big break. We never became super serious, but we got hot and heavy quickly.

It was fun, until a couple of months in, he started forgetting his wallet. Early in the dating, we'd alternate paying, like a normal couple did. Then once, he forgot his wallet. The first time we were out and he forgot it, I said, "No problem." The second time, okay. But the third time, well, I was getting a little curious. By the fourth time . . .

"

Lindsay – Well, don't forget you also got flea bites at his house. I don't think he was using his wallet much in general.

The fourth time I said, "Maybe we should consider getting you a man purse or something."

Each time, I paid the bill, and each time he would promise to pay me back. But he never did. It never happened. I assumed that he had been on a show and that show was canceled. He didn't immediately get another gig, and the money ran out while he was "between jobs."

Eventually, especially if we were out with other people, I just started putting my credit card out to pay. I didn't want to make a big thing of it for him. But that's not the strange part of this story.

Since the relationship was so much fun and going really well, we decided to make a little video.

> **Lindsay** – How well could it have been going if he kept stiffing you on the dinner bill?

Things were extremely passionate and it seemed like a good idea to make a . . . well, a sex tape. He was great in bed, and on one lazy day, we'd spent half the day in bed. One thing led to another and the idea of recording ourselves came up. He had all of the necessary equipment (an iPhone) and he knew what he was doing, so it seemed like a good idea at the time. Together, we were adventurous in bed. We thought it would be fun to watch. We used his phone to make it. He sent me a copy.

> **Lindsay** – Mistake number two.

One night after work, we were grabbing a drink. I had worked late and didn't have much time. He picked me up and we sat down for a quick one. At that point, the relationship had begun to go sour a bit. That's what worried me. It had been great at one point and we made the video during happy times, but when things started to slow down and it became apparent we didn't have a future together, well, that's when I started having sleepless, panicked nights that I was going to wake up and see that my tape was online.

> **Lindsay** – And that's why you don't make sex tapes. Especially on his equipment.

"Listen," I said. "I don't know why, but I'm really panicking about the video." A lot of people's phones had been hacked around that time. "I don't want it leaked if you get hacked. I don't want this out there. Can you delete it?"

He refused. Worse, he got really upset, grabbed his phone, walked out of the bar, and went to his car and left. I called and texted him for weeks, begging him to delete the video. His answers were weird. "Who do you think I am? A convict or something? Why is this such a big deal? I would never do anything with the video."

I thought, *then just delete it!*

The fact that he would not worried me even more. We broke up over the fact that he wouldn't delete the tape in front of me. That signified the end for me—that he didn't care enough to make me feel comfortable about it all. The trust went out the window. I clearly couldn't trust him to have my back, let alone pay for his own dinner.

Eventually, he said he did delete the video. I was concerned that because of the fact that he clearly had no money, he'd get desperate enough to try to make some money off of the video. I've never seen proof that it was killed.

> **Lindsay** – You can't say I didn't warn you. There better not be other sex tapes.

Well. . . .

The Over-Analyzation

Karina

The lesson I learned was to use an actual camera and tape for your next sex tape, so you can destroy it. The phone, well, that was a bad idea. Also, make sure your "co-star" is as famous or more famous, so he has something to lose as well if it is released. Not that I'm making any more tapes.

As for the guy with the phone tape, I haven't seen him pop up anywhere lately, but I hope he's making a living being in an actual show or film.

Lindsay

If you're going to make a sex tape, you should always be the sole owner of the footage, plain and simple. Why risk it unless you want it to get seen?

Guy's Corner

Ricardo

Well, deep inside, I bet there is a little tiny part of Karina that is thinking right now she would not mind that video maybe being seen by people.

Ralph

This is someone who obviously knows that Karina is successful and has some money and is just hanging on that. That seems as clear as day to me. Forget your wallet once, well, then you forgot your wallet, but you can't forget your wallet more than once. That's it.

Lindsay and Karina

Sometimes, when we are out for drinks with our friends, it's almost a contest to see who has the best dating disaster of the week. We dish on everything that's gone wrong and also love hearing about the ones that go right. We're all in this together, and at the end of the day, life without laughter isn't a life well lived. The next story, told by Lindsay's sister, has made it into our happy hour chats many, many times. It's definitely one for the books and reminds us of just how insane some people really are.

Taco Boy

Lori, Lindsay's Sister, Portland, OR

When I laugh about this date with my friends, I refer to the guy as Taco Boy. I met him shortly after I moved to Portland, Oregon. I didn't know very many people, so I decided online dating would be a good way to meet some. This guy was a freelance photographer, or at least that's what he said in his profile. His picture made him look cute. Once we connected, we e-mailed back and forth a lot. He seemed like a really nice guy, and it appeared as though we had some common interests—music, sci-fi, and I also liked taking pictures in my spare time. It's difficult to get to know anyone over e-mail, but I felt like I had a good vibe for this guy and knew him well enough by the time we decided to go out. All indications were that he was sweet, though I was fully aware that I wouldn't know for sure until I actually spoke to him in person and got to see his facial expressions and personality.

> **Lindsay** – I definitely think a phone date before an in-person date can save you a lot of time, but my sister

hates the phone, so I can't dock her for the straight-to-date approach.

He lived in a neighboring town called Beaverton. We decided to meet up in downtown Portland. He told me he didn't drive or didn't have a car or something like that, and that he would take our MAX light rail system to get in. We met at a cool and popular brewery called Deschutes Brewery. He arrived before me and had ordered a beer for himself while he waited in a big bar area. When I walked in, he looked like his picture. Totally normal, cute, and well groomed. Since our date was at 8:00 p.m., I thought it was a dinner date, though we hadn't really discussed that.

> *Karina* – I'm pretty sure the rule on these things is to be clear it is a drinks-only date, but if you like the guy, then go ahead and have dinner. But you don't want to get locked into a meal if you're with a dud. Not to mention, my mom always told me never to go on a date hungry. You never know if there is going to be food. And second, it's not ladylike to stuff your face on the first date. That's probably somewhat of an old-fashioned way of thinking, but I can promise that it has actually worked for me.

I sat down and we started talking. I ordered a glass of wine. We were chatting with sort of light conversation at first, but the conversation quickly turned to weirder topics. Too quickly, in fact. He told me that he lived in an apartment and that he didn't sleep in his bedroom.

"Oh, okay, so your bed is in your living room?" I asked.

"No, I have a mat," he said. "I sleep on a mat."

I'm thinking: *A camping mat? Strange. But if it's comfortable, I guess that's cool and maybe interesting.*

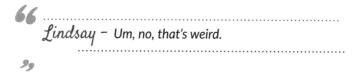

Lindsay - Um, no, that's weird.

I nodded and played along. Then he explained that, ideally, he would like to weave his own mat. He wanted it to be Japanese style and he wanted to attach it to a cot sort of frame. He'd given this a lot of thought and had a very specific plan and idea.

Karina - I would say a little too much thought. Who knows, maybe he had back problems and sleeping on a hard mat was helping him. At the same time, there is such a thing as an extra firm mattress. Having traveled to Japan many times, I too had an urge to experience sleeping Japanese style on a straw mat. And let me tell you, the art of lovemaking on one of those definitely requires a good deal of unconventional experimentation. For the most part, most of the Kama Sutra positions are either impossible or painful, and rug burns don't just take your skin off but also leave you with slivers. Even though the magic carpet delivers by flying you to your desired place, with a tatami mat the destination might be not as desirable.

I wanted to be part of the conversation and polite, so I said something about how his biggest challenge might be tying off the weave around the bed and having it be strong enough to lie on. He got defensive and, in fact, angry with me and was very clear it wouldn't be a problem at all. It was strange that it got so heated so quickly, but also strange that he immediately veered off into talking about where he lived and how he lived. He wanted to talk about the mat thing; that was obvious.

66

Lindsay – *Strange that he'd be so into his mat yet defensive about it at the same time. Seems like he's got some serious baggage along with that mat.*

He still seemed nice, just a little quirky. I figured, whatever. Since there was a menu in front of each of us, I decided to switch the topic of conversation to what I thought would be a little easier and have less potential for weirdness. I looked at it and said, "Maybe I'll get this . . . or that. What are you going to get?"

"I already ate," he said.

"Oh, I'm sorry. Given the hour I just assumed we were eating."

"No, I stopped at a taco cart on my way from the MAX while I was walking here. I got some tacos. I have an extra taco in my backpack if you want it."

66

Karina – *Run. And run fast! Let's start with the backpack. Weren't backpacks popular in the '80s and '90s? Or when we were still in school? Or camping? Not sure I've ever seen anyone pack a backpack for a date. What else does he hide in there? And was that taco just randomly floating around in it? It's a date, not an episode of Survivor.*

This guy wanted me to eat it at the restaurant—food he had brought in from elsewhere, probably all squished up in his backpack from an hour ago.

I politely explained that I wasn't so much in the mood for tacos, but that I was hungry. He suggested we leave and go to a really great pizza place nearby. I agreed, though I thought it strange he wanted to eat pizza since he had just told me he didn't want to eat at all. At this point in the date, I was done. I knew there was no chance I was going on a second date, but I'm sort of an overly polite person and I was hungry, so I agreed to leave the bar and head to the pizza place. I figured that was the best bet for a quick exit strategy because pizza was fast. I do tend to just stick things out; this was one of those things. He was a little sad, a little rude, and obviously weird, but I wanted to make the best of the situation, get a slice, and go home. I didn't feel threatened by him or anything like that; in fact, he was so little I could have beaten him up.

No, he didn't pay for my drink. We paid separately. At that point, I didn't care. I was hungry and I wanted to leave. I'm hypoglycemic so when my blood sugar gets low I'm just like, "All right, let's eat." We closed out the tab and went down the road to the pizza place. We walked there. It was close. It turned out to be very cute, too. One of those mellow, but nice, places where you walk up, order, and pay, but then they bring it to you. I ordered a plain slice. Just cheese pizza. That was all that I felt like. After I gave my order, I looked over to him to see what he was getting. I assumed he had let me order first to be polite.

"What are you going to get?" I asked.

"Oh, I'm not going to get anything."

This was getting weirder to me by the second, but I just wanted my freaking pizza and then I wanted to leave. I didn't even want to talk to him anymore. We sat down and I had nothing to say, so it was slightly awkward, but within minutes my slice came and I felt immediately better. It wasn't a huge slice. Just a normal slice of pizza. I was just getting set to pick it up and take a bite, when he asked, "Oh, can I have half of that?"

Without even saying one word, I tore it in half and handed it to him. I kept thinking, *just get me out of here.* I ate my pizza in practically four bites and then made up an excuse about having to get up early, so I needed to hit the road. He was floored I was wrapping it up so quickly, since he'd taken the time to take the MAX all the way in to meet with me. I stuck to my guns, though, and offered to drive him to the station, insisting I had a big meeting in the morning that I had to fly out for. I felt bad. It was still light out as I was wrapping it up. The truth was, I was going to go and meet friends after the date anyway, so I was just going to get there much earlier than expected.

We walked to my car and he got in. I looked at him and said, "I'm new to town. You'll have to tell me how to get to the station."

"How can you not know how to get to the station?" he asked.

"Well, aside from the fact that I'm new, I drive," I explained.

He got me there, and when he was getting out he said, "I'll call you." Not that I ever wanted to hear from him again. He didn't call.

I learned a lot from the date. When someone starts talking about thatching his own mat to sleep on in his living room, you're probably done. You probably don't need to continue the date. That, combined with the fact that he was carrying a dirty old backpack, could have meant he was actually homeless. Also, when someone offers you a taco from that sad filthy backpack, politely refuse and get the hell out. Back away slowly. And third, if someone wants to take you out to pizza after offering backpack tacos, make sure he orders his pizza first. That's just to make sure he's getting some and you won't have to share yours.

Best Worst Pickup Lines Ever

(Yes! These really happened.)

I'm sorry, but you owe me a drink. (Why?) Because when I looked at you, I dropped mine.

. . . .

Can I have directions? (To where?) To your heart.

. . . .

Can I take a picture of you to prove to all my friends that angels do exist?

. . . .

Your body is about 70 percent water and I'm thirsty.

. . . .

Was your dad a boxer? Because you're a knockout.

. . . .

Are you from Tennessee? 'Cause, baby, you're the only ten I see!

. . . .

There's something wrong with my cell phone. It doesn't have your number in it.

. . . .

Excuse me, I think I dropped something. My jaw!!!

. . . .

Excuse me, I think you might have something in your eye. Oh wait, it's just a sparkle.

. . . .

I bet you $100 you're going to turn me down.

. . . .

I wish you were soap so I could feel you all over me.

. . . .

Do you work for UPS? 'Cause I swear I saw you check out my package.

. . . .

I think it's time I tell you what people are saying behind your back. "Nice ass!"

Lindsay and Karina

Not only did Lori meet Taco Boy, she met Sausage Boy. And not in a good way. We've decided she should no longer date guys with any food associations. Or who are also compulsive cheapskates.

Sausage Boy

Lori, Lindsay's Sister, Portland, OR

Talk about a bad dating streak. Shortly after my encounter with Taco Boy, I was hanging out in a bar with some friends. I started talking to a guy who seemed like a real sweetheart. He was funny, and since we were both in a lighthearted mood after a drink or two, it seemed like a good idea to hang out with him at the bar. My judgment wasn't skewed—he really appeared to be an okay guy.

He told me that his family ran a sausage business. "I help distribute the sausages and I make all of the sausage sauce," he said.

"In your kitchen at home?" I asked.

"Yeah, in my kitchen at home."

"Wow, very cool. That's great."

> **Karina –** It's either a very small sausage distribution or a very large kitchen. I think considering how Taco Boy turned out, maybe you should stay away from guys with food connotations.

A quick chat during happy hour turned into a great conversation and a later night than expected. After an hour or maybe more, he asked me what my favorite food was. I thought about it for a moment and then declared filet mignon my fave.

"What if I made you filet mignon?" he asked.

"You're going to cook for me?" I replied.

"Yes, come to my house next weekend, and I will make you filet mignon."

I left the bar that night psyched to have met someone cool. Later in the week, he did follow up and we made a plan to meet at his house that weekend. We'd talked a bit about my dog and he had told me to bring him along. Which I thought was very cool. What I didn't learn until I was getting ready to go that night was that he lived super, super far outside of Portland. He told me approximately where to go—the name of his neighborhood—but said to call him once I got close and he'd give me directions. It seemed like a very flawed plan, and I realized it was going to take me a while to get out there.

Once I got close, I called him.

"Hey," I said. "I don't have your address yet. I'll pull over and punch it into my phone and map it."

"No, no, no, just stay on the line. I'll walk you in."

"Wait, no. I think the address would be easier, because there's a lot of traffic."

He ended up giving me directions and repeatedly getting me turned around. He mixed up left turns with right turns and it was sort of a disaster.

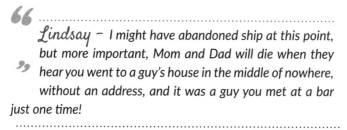

Lindsay – I might have abandoned ship at this point, but more important, Mom and Dad will die when they hear you went to a guy's house in the middle of nowhere, without an address, and it was a guy you met at a bar just one time!

I felt bad so I stayed the course. I was hoping at the very least it would be fun for my dog, even though it was super annoying. It wasn't deal-breaker territory at all. This guy was just dumb with directions.

I finally got to his house. The house looked okay from the outside, but the way he answered the door—all disgusting and sweaty—was a bit alarming. He told me he had been vacuuming. When I stepped in, it was clear he hadn't done much cleaning at all. His house was dirty. It was super dirty. The carpet was gross and there was just crap everywhere, and honestly, vacuuming would not have made a difference. It was a dirty house.

I hesitated a little because I was so grossed out. I wasn't nervous, but it wasn't nice. But my dog ran in so I thought, *Okay, crap. Well, let's just see what happens.* What happened was the dirt got worse as I went deeper into the house. The sink was full of filthy pots and pans. There were boxes of crap against almost every wall. It felt almost claustrophobic in there. Add to that he was sweaty and disgusting because he was in a hurry to clean his house, which, by the way, needed professional cleaners. It did not need one guy vacuuming.

"Do you mind if I take a quick shower?" he asked.

I absolutely didn't mind. This guy smelled bad. "No, please, go ahead."

Karina – *I think at the bare minimum a guy should be able to get ready before the date. Like showering at least. I've read that smell is the strongest sense of our memory and one's personal scent, pheromones, is what attracts people to each other. And more than that, it is believed that when you choose perfume or cologne, it should complement your natural pheromones for the ultimate level of seduction. Maybe Sausage Boy wanted to make sure he nailed that part in and kept all of his pheromones out on a display. Not to mention, I bet he wanted to showcase to Lori that he's very handy at home and is an expert with a vacuum. And as for his intricate yet adventurous sense of direction and navigation, he'll be able to navigate her through life like a captain. He is a catch. What's there not to like? Marriage material. Looks like his sausage means business.*

There I was, sitting in his house. My dog was somewhere in the yard playing with his dog. (At least they were getting along great, so someone was having fun.) I sat there for more than half an hour reading a magazine. This guy didn't strike me as a fancy guy at all, so what could possibly have taken him so long? I finally flipped on the TV, and after a few minutes, he came out.

"I'll get the grill going," he said.

"Great," I said.

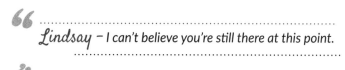

Lindsay – I can't believe you're still there at this point.

We walked out back and he lit up a very tiny little camping grill with a small propane can you screw on. It was something you might be able to heat a can of beans on, not grill steak. There was no BBQ. Just this joke of a travel-sized "grill."

He lit the "grill," dropped the steaks onto it, and then said, "We should go inside."

"Shouldn't we stay out here? I like my steak rare, so it won't take too long."

"No, we're fine. We'll wait inside. It's going to take a bit."

So we hung out inside, playing with the dogs, and a lot of time passed. He hadn't gone out to flip the steaks or check on them. And they weren't huge pieces of meat. These were small round steaks.

Once again, not wanting to seem too pushy or anything, I suggested we take a look. And once again, he insisted the steaks didn't need to come in yet, that they would be fine and weren't ready. The TV was on and we were chatting, but I was antsy. And hungry, of course. I'm always hungry. Finally, I put my foot down.

"Dude, you need to go out and check on the steak. It's going to be very well done."

He said okay, but he didn't immediately move.

"Seriously," I said again. "You need to check on it."

It was burnt completely to a crisp. There were two little charred balls of black meat sitting on the plate when he came back in. Burnt, crusty, charred blackness. They were the saddest steaks I'd ever seen.

"Wow," he said. "Sorry."

"We can't eat that," I said.

"Maybe the dogs will eat it."

> *Lindsay* – I'm sorry, this is certainly a disaster, but it's hilarious. I can just picture Lori starving, looking forward to her steak, and then as the minutes roll by, her hopes of a good dinner deteriorate and she's left with an inedible piece of rubber. I've seen my sister hungry and, let's just say, starving her won't win her over. It could actually put you in danger. Watch out, Sausage Boy. Speaking of that, where were all the sausages?

I asked him if he had anything else we could eat and he said no. There was nothing to go with the steak, no side dishes, no back-up food, no cereal. Nothing. At the very least, I would have thought there would have been some sausage and sauce in the freezer, since that's what this guy made for a living. It was the craziest, emptiest kitchen on the planet, considering his family business.

"Well, thanks so much," I said. "But I have to go. I'm sorry. I'm hungry. But I appreciate the effort."

I took my dog and I left. I couldn't even believe that had happened. This was just after the Taco Boy non-date. With Sausage Boy, I at least assumed, as an actual sausage boy due to lineage, he'd have some food around. At least have some sausages in the fridge. This poor guy kept texting me afterward, asking me if I was still interested. I explained to him that it probably wasn't meant to be, which didn't stop him. Worse, he couldn't understand why I wasn't into him. So, that was it for food people for me.

Grooming Gone Wrong

We've all had it happen: We primp and prep and get ready to look our most fabulous, but something goes terribly wrong.

I bought this scented powder that smelled fantastic. I had a big date that night, so I put a little behind my ears, in my cleavage, and . . . well . . . down there. Somehow, my chemistry and the smell in the *down there* area didn't match, and a horrible odor emerged. I didn't realize it until it was too late. As my date and I walked, every time the wind blew, a rather repulsive odor emerged. —*Lindsay*

A bikini wax was in order for a fourth date of mine. It quickly became clear that the waxer was doing her first wax ever. She spilled wax on hair that didn't need to get removed. I had to peel my panties off at home, pop a squat in the bathtub for an hour to soak off the rogue wax, and, in the end, cut out large swaths of waxy hair. It looked like a Picasso down there. Lights out on the date. —*Stacy*

I went to a hair salon to get a blowout before a date I was really excited about. My regular stylist, Ricardo, was in Brazil, so I was forced to try someone else for a quick blow-dry. I'm not sure what kind of shampoo they used, but my head did not like it. It immediately turned red, and within hours it looked like there was snow on top of my head. Mortified and rife with the dandruff from the shampoo, I was terrified that my date would be equally disgusted. I decided to wash my hair again with my own shampoo and condition it with a scalp mask. It was risky because the date was an hour away, but I couldn't go with a head full of flakes. Unfortunately, the scalp condition only got worse because I was evidently allergic to the shampoo the salon had used. I dried my hair with cool air, knowing the hot air would make my scalp worse. I hoped that I would be good to go if I just shook my head upside down a few times. I wasn't. My date arrived not long after, and I resorted to wearing a hat. It was a bit awkward because it was summertime. It was hot and my hat was more for the winter or fall, but I rocked it and refused to take it off until I got home that night. Never again will I get blown out by anyone but Ricardo or someone he personally refers. —*Lindsay*

. . . .

Chapter 5:
The Crier

So Hot My Lips Bled, Like . . . Literally

Lindsay

What are friends for if not to pass along a date to you when they think you're a better match for a guy? That's what Karina did for me.

> *Karina* – *Okay, it's not what it sounds like. This guy seemed truly incredible. He had great energy, a great smile, and he was intelligent, strong-minded, and confident. He was even just a little shy. But, of course, timing is everything. And in my particular situation, the timing was off. But great guys don't come along all too often. As I was talking to him, I realized that he might be a perfect match for my bestie, so I told him as much. I wasn't sure if he'd think I was crazy, but I explained I was still trying to get over someone, but I had a great friend who might be a match. I thought he'd entered my life for a reason. Maybe this was cupid's sarcastic way of bringing Lindsay and this guy together. Love works in mysterious ways. My pitch was very well received. Nailed it!*

It might sound a little strange, but Karina went on a date with a guy she was set up with. He'd been split from his wife for a year. He had two kids. She called me when the date ended for our usual date play-by-play.

"So," I asked, "what did you think of him?"

"Well," she said, "he was great. Amazing, in fact. Super sweet, super nice."

"I feel like there's a 'but' coming here," I said.

> 66
>
> *Karina* – There's almost always a "but"! Now, part two of the pitch: I've never done this before, but in my mind I thought I had hit the jackpot and I was going to be the maid of honor in their wedding. Yes, I know, I move quickly, but you know what, who has time to waste? So I delivered the pitch to Lindsay, and now she was equally as excited as I was.

"Well, he was nice, but there's something else."

"Tell me!"

"I actually think you guys would make a way better couple than he and I," she said.

I was a little shocked. I thought about it for a minute and said, "That's interesting."

"Would you be open to it?" she asked.

"If you, my best friend, are saying that you think there might be a love match, I'm going to trust your instinct and I'll be open to going on a date with him."

She told me that she thought he was a great dad and really grounded. Since I'm a single mom, based on everything she told me, it seemed to make sense actually. She thought personality wise that he was strong but also sensitive and kind.

I went with her advice and met up with him for a first date. He worked in finance and had a son and daughter. That was all that I knew. And, obviously, Karina's recommendation held a lot of weight. We met for dinner. What I learned on my own was that he had a good head on his shoulders and seemed solid. We had a nice conversation. I'm not sure if I felt chemistry with him on that date, but I have a three-date rule. If there's a positive vibe and no reason not to go out again, and the guy seems nice and legit, I try to give him three dates to see what emerges.

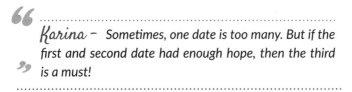

Karina – Sometimes, one date is too many. But if the first and second date had enough hope, then the third is a must!

What I did find attractive was the fact that he seemed to be an amazing dad. He was nervous on the first date—that was clear—and maybe inhibited a bit, but he was worth the second date for sure. The second date initially felt like the first date. There was no progression at first. It was pleasant, cordial, and full of good conversation. I started to think, *Okay, maybe this guy will just be a friend of mine.* In fairness, it was a brief date. Instead of dinner, we met for a drink because Karina and I had a premiere to attend. I had suggested a drink afterward. He had already been out for dinner and was drinking before he came to the second date. When I arrived, I initially didn't realize that he was already pretty plastered. He hid it well. We started talking—just small talk, but interesting conversation, just like our first date. Then we got on to the topic of our kids.

That day, he had received some sort of emergency call from his ex. It wasn't serious, but it was out of the ordinary to hear from her during the day when she had the kids. He also mentioned that he was concerned she wasn't a great mother. He said they handled things differently, that she was selfish, and that their parenting styles weren't the same. Suddenly, in the middle of this sort of nonchalant discussion, he became emotional. He admitted how tough it was. I was trying to be sensitive to it and the shift our date had taken when suddenly he just started crying. There was a floodgate of tears. I wasn't sure what I was supposed to do, and while I appreciated that he loved his kids and that was beautiful, the tears on date two were kind of a turnoff. It was weird. I thought it was strange that he couldn't pull it together. If he couldn't pull it together on date two, I wondered if he'd be able to get into the space to be able to date people, or if maybe it was just too soon for him. Regardless, I sat and listened to him. He apologized for crying and felt badly about it all. He asked if I wanted a second drink when he got it together.

Then he revealed he was sloshed, that he'd had a ton to drink before we met. I declined the second drink and went home. I didn't address the future even when he continued to ask if he could see me again soon.

The next day, he called me and was profusely apologetic. "I don't normally cry on dates and I can't believe I did. Perhaps it's because I feel so comfortable around you."

He seemed genuine and sincere so I reverted to my three-date rule and agreed, when asked, to give this guy one more chance. My mom always said it's not about the initial chemistry right off the bat and to look for the guys who seem capable of being your rock. She reminded me that relationships grow over time. Three dates usually show me if rock status is an option.

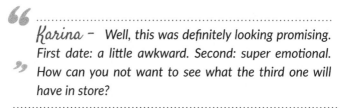

Karina – *Well, this was definitely looking promising. First date: a little awkward. Second: super emotional. How can you not want to see what the third one will have in store?*

This guy's explanation made me feel comfortable, and I was okay with how badly he felt. So I went for it. My soft spot is when children are involved. I mean, this guy cried because he loved his kids so much. That wasn't a crime or a horrible quality. It was good. What I was worried about was chemistry. Did I want this guy to touch me? Kiss me? That was unclear. It needed to be clear by the end of date three, that much I knew.

He took me to Katsuya in Brentwood. I first parked at his place and then we walked to dinner. I was prepared for an invite up after dinner, and I felt comfortable with that. If I had any hesitation, then I would have driven and met him there. But we enjoyed each other's company and our phone conversation was good, so I was cool with the plan for date three.

He was wearing a cashmere turquoise sweater, a very thin material, with nice blue jeans. I hadn't noticed before, but on date three I realized he had beautiful blue-green eyes. And during our conversation, talking about many different things, at a certain point he then disclosed that he'd had cancer at one point in his life, but that all was good and he was in remission. It became apparent that he was an incredible person really.

We walked back to his apartment (sort of a townhouse). I went upstairs and he offered me wine. I said, "Sure, I'll take a glass of wine." But before he went to retrieve it, he grabbed me and started making out with me. And it was actually quite good. I must say, I was completely surprised. He was assertive, which was nice, because I had begun to wonder if he had it in him. He did. After kissing for a few seconds, he picked me up and locked my legs around his waist, and we kept kissing and kissing and kissing. He put me against the wall and continued kissing me. Then he took me into his bedroom, threw me on the bed, and we kissed some more. He kissed my neck, he kissed my arms—it was very hot, but still third date material. He took off his shirt, I didn't take off mine, but it was becoming very passionate and went on for quite some time. Suddenly, in the middle of the passion and kissing, I started to taste blood. I tried to ignore it, thinking it was my imagination, but then my lips started to pulsate, the feeling that happens when something is severely swollen. I wasn't sure what to do. I'd never been in that situation before. I wasn't sure what to say since it was in the middle of the heat of the moment.

"Um, I think I taste blood, do you taste blood?" I finally stopped to ask.

He couldn't tell in the dark, so he got up to turn on the light. Then he gasped. "Oh, my gosh. Oh, my gosh! Are you okay?"

"What? What's wrong?" I asked. Before I could get up to look, he bolted out of the room and said he was getting ice.

"Your lips are totally swollen and bleeding. I feel terrible."

I put the ice on for a while and then got up to look in the mirror. It was a bit unclear as to what exactly had happened, but he had been kissing me so passionately and sucking my lips and all of that, and I guess it was too much for my lips to handle. They were literally bleeding. We did have a great laugh about it while I iced. Of course, at this point I was sort of over it all, but I looked down and realized that in the middle of all of this, he was still completely turned on. He was so hard at that point that it was sticking straight out, even though he had clothes on. Straight like a coat rack almost. He was sweet about it all and took really good care of me. But I'd never had that happen to me before. Ever.

That was basically the end of that. Once we stopped, I realized that even though he was raring to go, I was still in too much pain. I couldn't do anything and I just wanted to go home. So I did. On my way home I had to think about what I would tell my son. First thought was that I got mugged, but of course that's totally inappropriate for a little guy so I came up with the most believable story I could think of. The next morning Royce said, "Mommy, what happened to your lips?" My reply: "Mommy had to go to the bathroom in the middle of the night and it was so dark that I walked into the wall on my way to the bathroom." He bought it, phew!

We never did progress after that. I saw him again, and he kissed me very gently this time, but the timing was off. It was just one of those things. He had a trip and I had a trip, so by the end of all of that, it sort of fizzled. Truth be told: While I was away that time I met another guy and I kind of wound up liking him more. The chemistry was immediate and basically evaporated anything I'd felt for the guy who gave me swollen lips. I had no interest by the time I returned. We let it drift away, and I've never had swollen lips since.

— The Over-Analyzation —

Karina

Oh Lord, the cry baby. I'm sure this will make me sound like a cold-hearted beeyatch, but it reminds me of one of the first lessons I learned when my family moved to the States: When you are asked, "How are you?" people don't really expect you to give them an answer. They don't want to hear your problems. When you are on a date, and date number two at that, there is nothing wrong with talking about each other—actually, that's exactly what you are supposed to do—but maybe don't dig too deeply into the trenches and unleash the tears. Don't get me wrong: If you are on a date at the movies, and you are both tearing up, that's a sign of sensitivity. A couple of tears from a man—not a bad thing. But when the tears come out before you know how to spell his last name (and are a result of him feeling pity for himself!), well, then you might be fighting for the "queen" throne in the relationship. And as for the lips, well, at least you got a free lip job!

Lindsay

This is one of my favorite dating stories. I still have the pictures to prove it, since most people think that it's entirely made up. Also, after a couple of days, the scab was almost gone and my lips actually looked quite amazing. It made me think for a nanosecond about getting my lips done. Then I thought, *maybe I should just find another guy to give me a lip job like this one. No needles, no cost, not bad!*

Guy's Corner

Ralph

There's a sense of vulnerability and sensitivity in the character himself. That's okay. But obviously in the rules of passion, bleeding lips are on a whole new level. I've never kissed a woman hard enough to make her lips bleed. I'm jealous, though I don't know if that's a good thing. Maybe I should give it my best shot with my wife.

Ricardo

Listen, I'm all about being emotional. But I think he was just being overly sentimental because he wanted to get laid.

Don't Cry Over Spilled Gummy Bears

Karina

I like a nice gift just as much as the next girl. Who doesn't like being thought of? But spending money on gifts certainly is not everything—I don't put a lot of weight on that sort of thing. I can buy my own stuff. I don't want to support a guy, but I'd like an equal.

> *Lindsay* – Still, if you're going to spend the time buying a girl a gift, you've got to give it a little thought.

Money isn't ever a deciding factor, and I don't need to be showered with jewels and bags. Still, when I'm dating a millionaire, a nice and thoughtful gift (not expensive) is sweet.

The date was a setup by a mutual friend. He lived in Colorado. He'd been married before, had a couple of kids, and was a little bit older than me. He was super good-looking and a brilliant businessman. He made his first million in high school selling strawberries, essentially. He went on from there doing several clever deals and projects.

Sometimes with that kind of money, eccentricity follows. At times, he would treat me like an employee, and frequently I'd have to stop him to explain that it wasn't appropriate for a guy to talk to his girlfriend that way. I helped him understand that. I helped him with the way he dressed, too, making him a little more casual away from work and his business attire comfort zone. He wasn't like Richard Gere–*Pretty Woman* dressing, but he was plain. I gave him some zing. Eventually, he was calling me saying he'd spent a ton of money at

John Varvatos. And then he would model his new acquisitions for me. I enjoyed being creative with his wardrobe.

I wasn't offended, but I found it strange that he'd come to LA, drop $5,000 on clothing for himself, and only bring me two individual chocolates, once on a piece of paper. A paper napkin, to be exact. Not a box of something fancy, just a couple of individual Godivas that maybe were free at the store or something. It was weird.

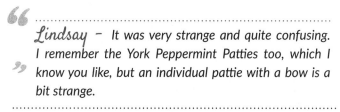

Lindsay – It was very strange and quite confusing. I remember the York Peppermint Patties too, which I know you like, but an individual pattie with a bow is a bit strange.

Now, we'd met months before and he hadn't stepped up to the plate after one date. He had said, "You're so *amazing* . . . you're an *amazing* person," but after that one date, he didn't ask me out again. For a long time afterward, if someone said "amazing," I asked them to choose a different adjective. Once he made this big deal about picking out three mystery gifts for me from a small boutique for Valentine's Day. He was hyped up about it and made a point to tell me about it a few times. He was excited. And frankly, so was I. It was, as he liked to put it, *amazing*.

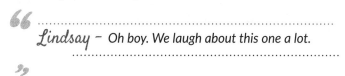

Lindsay – Oh boy. We laugh about this one a lot.

The first gift arrived at my house. It was a single bar of soap. Granted, it wasn't Dove, but it wasn't artisanal or anything special. Just a bar of soap. Naturally, I smelled myself in fear of him giving me a hint. At first, I was mortified, but after thanking him for the first present and talking to him, he revealed that it was his favorite type of soap. And he wanted to share that with me. *Umm, okay. Thank you, I guess.*

> *Lindsay* – I would chisel that apart to see if a bracelet was inside. We thought the soap was the lead-up to something big. Like part three of the gift was going to be something big and the soap was a hint. We figured there would be a grand finale.

The second mystery gift was a very inexpensive pair of flea market-ish metal wire earrings. Aside from the fact that I'm allergic to that kind of metal in my ears and it makes my lobes turn black, if he knew me at all, he would know they were never something I would wear. They were man-made out of wire. I thought, *These are re-gifters. Maybe one of the kids at my studio would like them.* At this point, I thought that he was probably playing it down so he could shock and surprise me (a relatively difficult task) with the third and final gift.

Next came the grand finale—the highlight of all of the gifts. It was shipped from Colorado, so to be clear, I was certain the shipping cost more than the gift itself. It was yellow gummy bears in a glass jar. Gummy bears, the candy. In a plain glass mason jar. There was no sweet note, no other surprise, nothing. If you know me at all (clearly he didn't), you know my choice of sugar intake is dark chocolate.

> *Lindsay* – Maybe he mixed up his gift for one that was supposed to go to his daughter? Gosh, I hope she didn't get what I would have imagined a man to buy for a woman as a surprise.

It was so weird. He even had the weird nerve to call and ask me: "Did you try the gummy bears? Aren't they amazing?"

Was this guy baiting me for some kind of argument? I didn't even know what to say. I called my mom to get some motherly wisdom and all she could say was, "Wow, he is master of originality." What was I missing? There must have been at least a card saying sweet things or something, so I tore the package apart looking. Nothing. Just the jar of candy.

"Well, to be honest, I'm not a gummy bear person. I love dark chocolate—with filling, without filling, with nuts, whatever. But gummy bears aren't my thing. I gave some to the kids at the studio. But thank you. It was a nice gesture." A couple of weeks later he came out to see me again and saw the jar at my place. He was genuinely excited that I saved some for him. *What? Really?* And as he ate one, he said, "Well, these are the best gummy bears I've had." Personally, I had no clue that there is a range from bad to amazing in the field of gummy bears. To my knowledge, the only difference is the color, but apparently this special order was the top of the line. So I tried one more to see if finally the gummy bear would start a Mardi Gras in my mouth. Nothing.

Months later, after a long silence period, he came to LA. He wanted to take me to dinner. I thought, *what the heck, let me entertain this* amazing *man.* We went to dinner and we had a good time. At one point, instead of "amazing," he said, "You know what, it's so weird, I love everything about you. I love the way you carry yourself, the way you talk, the way you look, everything."

I was in a weird place, so I came off very harsh at the time. But later I thought that if a man could say those things, then maybe I should date him. I tried, but then came the gummy bears.

I tried to hang in there. I was on the East Coast for work. Generally, I try not to mix work and relationships together, because then it gets into a gray area where they tell you how to handle your business. If you don't listen and handle things as they suggest, or the way they see it, then they pull that "Oh, you don't want my opinion" attitude. So I try to keep it separate. Still, he came for a couple of days to meet me, knowing I had to work.

He was waiting for me at a hotel. I told him I needed to knock out a couple of hours of work, but that I'd be there right after that. I didn't invite him to my work. Work is work. He wouldn't take me to a business deal or his office, so why would I take him to my office, the dance studio?

He felt that I was trying to hide him for whatever reason. I met him afterward at a restaurant. We ordered food. I said, "Listen, I need to send one text to my boss to let her know how everything is progressing at work. Sorry. I'll be very fast. Just give me one second,

so I can reply and get this cleared up and then I can focus on dinner."
I texted back and forth with my boss very quickly, addressing what
I thought of my part and the details of what we were working on.
Then I put my phone away and looked up, ready to enjoy dinner.

Across the table, this guy was crying. Actually, he was sobbing.
The tears were streaming down his face and falling onto the table.
"Dramatic" would be an understatement. It was the middle of the
day in a public restaurant. There weren't just tears in his eyes, there
were tears pouring down his cheeks. I assumed something bad had
happened to his family.

"Are you okay? What's wrong? What happened?" I asked.

"I don't think we're on the same page," he said. "I feel like you
don't feel about me the same way I do you."

"Wait, wait. What?" I was so confused. "I just needed to send
one text."

"We are at a restaurant eating dinner and you are on your
phone!" He was so upset.

*And you're crying about it? Major overreaction. Lord forbid I need to
send an e-mail.*

"Yes," I said. "I told you I needed to finish one bit of business.
I'm sorry. I'm so appreciative that you came to see me in Baltimore.
It was a nice surprise. And I'm loving our time together, but I have
to work. I can't just drop everything and cancel work to be available
to you."

It wasn't even a planned trip together. I was there to work. I had
even tried to cut rehearsal short to meet him and spend time with
him. *PS: Don't tell my boss.*

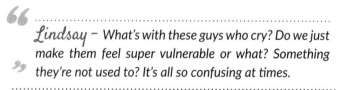

Lindsay – What's with these guys who cry? Do we just
make them feel super vulnerable or what? Something
they're not used to? It's all so confusing at times.

I have a pet peeve in relationships. If there's a problem, I like to
figure it out quickly. Find a solution and move on, not sit around and

talk about it for hours. If there's an issue, I like to fix it, but I don't like to analyze it. We went back to the hotel that night without resolution or a fix, mostly because there wasn't a problem. I was working. I also had to work again the next day, starting at 3:00 in the morning. I explained that to him—that I had to be on air at the morning show for 5:00 a.m.

"Can we go to sleep early? Otherwise, I get loopy on the air. That's not entertaining or my best look."

Well, we climbed into bed. But we didn't go to sleep. He wanted to talk. And talk. And talk. He talked all night until it was 3:00 a.m. and I had to head to the studio. That was a major breaking point for me, never mind the gummy bears. I'll take a truck-load of gummy bears over a conversation that leads nowhere. At this point, I was drained, exhausted, and ready to leave the hotel by jumping out of the window.

As I was leaving I said, "I'm so sorry, but there are certain behavioral patterns that I will never be okay with. If you love communication so much that you want to spend all night talking about you, well that's special, but it doesn't work for me. There is a time and place for everything, and here and now is not it."

I don't think he even wanted me to work, because nothing seemed good enough. He wanted all of my time and I just felt cornered, like I couldn't move or breathe. It was suffocating. That was the beginning of the end. It was disrespectful not to understand I had to work, too. He wasn't paying my bills, nor did I want him to. I appreciated the gesture of the dumb soap, and I never let on I was a prima donna who needed more. But his interfering in my work, not letting me do my work, well, that wasn't okay.

The Over-Analyzation
Karina

He always made it clear to me that he sought to understand (which is an *amazing* quality), so once the dust settled down, he also found an urge to let me understand what had happened, by sending me articles from *Cosmopolitan* magazine justifying and explaining why men cry and how this was a great thing and I should value it. Thanks, *Cosmopolitan*! Thank you!

Lindsay

Unfortunately, I think feeling out of control led to his strange behavior. He couldn't handle an equal or a partner and was looking for another employee. Problem is, the last person you put in a corner is Karina. Baby gets put in the corner before Karina.

Guy's Corner

Ricardo

Another crier? Wrong guy. And gummy bears? Really?

Lindsay and Karina

When we first heard this date we both needed to take a hot shower. Not for the usual seemingly good reasons, but because our skin was crawling. I'm still convinced she ended up in the ex-girlfriend's childhood bedroom. What a creep.

Just-When-You-Think-It-Can't-Get-Any-Worse Guy: A Mama's Boy (Sorta)

Martina, TV Producer, LA

This date went from gross to worse quickly. I moved to Hollywood and eventually wound up doing improv. I was working with several people in comedy at the time, one guy in particular that I found to be interesting and quirky and sexy and all of those things. I was free and clear of a boyfriend at the time, so when things started getting flirtatious with him, I thought I might as well play along. After rehearsal one night he said, "I'm house-sitting close by, why don't you come on over and we'll have a glass of wine and just sit and chat some more?" It sounded like a great idea so I said yes.

We went to this amazing home in a gorgeous neighborhood of Los Angeles. We built a fire, poured some wine, and sat on this beautiful big carpet in the living room. It was nice. Eventually, we started to kiss. Nothing crazy—our clothing remained on. Almost immediately, I felt uncomfortable. I wasn't sure exactly why, but something was bothering me. I looked down and realized we were both covered in fleas. They were everywhere—there were thousands of them. It was awful. We both jumped up, and before we normally would have at that stage, we took off all our clothes. We started shaking them furiously but realized we needed to do more to fix the situation. We took them to the dryer, threw everything in, and then took showers—separately, as we weren't at that point yet, and the bugs had certainly erased any chance of getting there just then. While we waited for our clothes, we both stood straight up on top of the bed—terrified to have our feet on the ground. Once we felt confident we'd gotten our clothes flea-free, we hopped, skipped, and jumped out of there. We were itchy still. Scratching ourselves as we fled.

"I'm not going to stay there tonight," he said. "I'm going to call my friends and let them know."

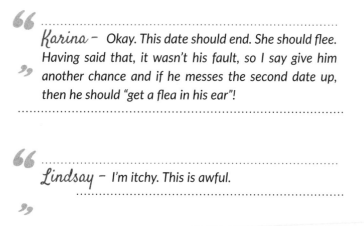

> *Karina* – Okay. This date should end. She should flee. Having said that, it wasn't his fault, so I say give him another chance and if he messes the second date up, then he should "get a flea in his ear"!

> *Lindsay* – I'm itchy. This is awful.

I knew it wasn't his fault. It was just an unfortunate and terrible, not to mention weird, way to start off the date. He asked me if I'd like to continue the date back at his place. I decided he was nice enough to give it a shot despite the infestation. His place wasn't far from bug central—both were in Hollywood, fifteen minutes or so apart. He pulled up and we walked around to the back of the house. He said, "Shhh. Be quiet. I have a roommate." Then we entered through a kitchen door, not the front. He said, "My roommate might be sleeping."

I agreed and whispered, "No problem." At first we didn't go beyond the kitchen. We sat and had a glass of wine and talked. He was nice. It was nice. Eventually we picked up where we'd left off at the house-sitting house and started kissing again. One thing led to another and eventually we found our way to his bedroom. I spent the night.

In the morning, early because it was still dark, I woke up. I hadn't really noticed the night before, but his bedroom was decorated like a kid's room. It had bright kid colors and posters and stuffed animals. Wearing just a T-shirt and underwear, I quietly got out of bed and made my way to the kitchen for a drink. I leaned against the counter, after I found a glass and water, and was smiling thinking about the night before. It had been weird, but nice. Suddenly, an eighty-year-old woman walked in, startling me. But she wasn't who I thought she was.

"Hello," I said. "I'm Martina. I'm so sorry. I'm here with your son, but I'll get out of your way and go back to his room. I don't want to be in your way. It's nice to meet you."

"Oh, don't worry," said the old woman. "And he's not my son."

I was confused. He had said roommate, but I couldn't imagine he was sharing a place with an eighty-year-old.

"He used to date my daughter," she finally said.

> *Karina* – Oh God. What? No way! He lived with his ex-girlfriend's mom? Wait, did they have a child and they slept in his or her room? Flee! Pull back. He might be a bloodsucking parasite.

> *Lindsay* – OMGosh, whose room were you in all night? Was it her childhood bedroom?

"What?" I said. "So, does he live here?"

"Yes," she said. "He does. When they broke up, he had no place to live so I took him in."

"So, I'm at his ex-girlfriend's mother's house."

"Yes," she said.

I walked back into the bedroom and asked him if he'd forgotten to mention anything to me.

He said, "Oh, you met my roommate? She's great. You'd really like her."

Bewildered, I explained to him that I had to leave. I got dressed, grabbed my stuff, and left.

Then it got even more bizarre.

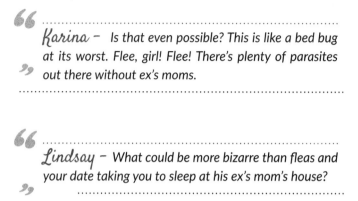

Karina – Is that even possible? This is like a bed bug at its worst. Flee, girl! Flee! There's plenty of parasites out there without ex's moms.

Lindsay – What could be more bizarre than fleas and your date taking you to sleep at his ex's mom's house?

There's an addendum to this story. Years later I was on location, working on a television show we were shooting. We were at Knott's Berry Farm. I was talking to some of the production staff there, and suddenly from way in the background, a clown with a microphone started shouting, "Martina, Martina." Then he was jumping up and down.

I was thinking, *what the fuck? How does a clown at Knott's Berry Farm know my name?*

It was him. It was flea-lives-with-his-ex's-mom guy. There was a sad clown ending to my terrible dating story.

Best Worst Pickup Lines Ever

(Yes! These really happened.)

You may be asked to leave soon. You're making the other women look bad.

. . . .

Would you grab my arm so I can tell my friends I've been touched by an angel?

. . . .

Of all the curves on your body, your smile is my favorite.

. . . .

Can I borrow your cell? I need to call animal control because I just saw a fox.

. . . .

I'm no organ donor but I'd be happy to give you my heart.

. . . .

If you're feeling down, I can feel you up.

. . . .

Do you believe in love at first sight or should I walk by again?

. . . .

See my friend over there? He wants to know if you think I'm cute.

. . . .

Chapter 6:
The Serial Cheater

He's Just Too F!@#able

Karina

Fans of *Dancing with the Stars* often wonder if pros and stars are hooking up. Sometimes they do, but not as often as you'd think. Usually, when the rumor mill is pumping hard and there are photos of everything a pair is doing—well, in most cases they're the ones who aren't sleeping together. But sometimes it happens. The heat intensifies when you're dancing. In my case, I had an instant attraction to someone on the show one season, and from there we dated for over two years. It was so instantly hot, I ignored a million little signs that screamed: *Don't do it. This relationship is wrong. This guy is a bad boy.*

He was a handsome guy. He walked into rehearsal for the first time and I thought, *Oh, wow. Hello.* It was obvious that we were both happy with the newly formed partnership. At the same time, we both wanted to be professional and therefore fought the feeling. That, and the fact that we were both in relationships at the time.

It all started out innocently. He would text me or call me. We'd chat or say things back and forth like, "I miss you." It elevated to him saying, "I can't wait to see you." Once, he texted me, maybe after a couple of drinks, and the interaction ended with, "Okay, I love you." That made meeting his girlfriend one week on set a little awkward, but that's the way it was. Around that same time, my relationship had become long distance, and on again off again, and the writing was on the wall with my new dance partner. I could feel what was happening, so I made a clean break with the boyfriend. My dance partner and I never discussed anything, but there was always that desire for one another. We never finished our rehearsals early.

One night, he asked me to meet him for dinner. He tested the waters first with a text to see if a date was potentially an option, then he picked up the phone and called to firm up the plan. I said yes, and he picked me up and took me to a hole-in-the-wall known for its great food. We talked for hours and had a great night. There was no kissing that night, but at the end of rehearsal the next day, when we were leaving, he leaned in and kissed me. We couldn't resist it anymore. We just went for it.

It was a steamy hot kiss, which was part of the problem. It was one of those relationships that I knew was wrong from the get-go, but I wanted to believe that it was different. But every warning was there: It was super hot, sexual, and exciting—wrong and right for all the wrong reasons. Don't get me wrong, I wish every woman could experience that kind of relationship, but just know, when it's steamy and crazy and exciting like that—make sure not to get hurt at the end. Those relationships usually end badly. I heard that one well-known producer once called my dance-partner-turned-boyfriend "too fuckable." That's what he was. He was a player and I saw it from miles away, but I didn't do anything. Deep down, we probably all want to tame a player. But we can't.

Still, despite all the signs—hearing him talk to other women on the phone in a way that screamed "romantically involved"—we moved in together after six months. For every skeptical move, he had a comprehensive explanation that left me feeling silly for questioning him. And the signs just kept coming. And I just kept believing him. I was totally gullible.

Once, when he returned from a trip, I was unpacking his suitcase and I found a bag of condoms in it. Not one or two, but about fifty or more of them. Why would a guy in a committed relationship need condoms when he traveled? I asked him just that. He said that he was holding them for a friend.

Lindsay – Because his friend was sixteen and he didn't want his mom to know? Or like when one of my past boyfriends said his brother needed him to bring him some from LA to NYC, where there's a twenty-four-hour Duane Reade on every corner. Come on!

I always believed him, of course, because I wanted to. And that was part me being dumb and part him always having these elaborate, colorful, well-thought-out, logical excuses for everything you called him on. He was so good at lying that he made me feel like a dumbass for questioning him. He had it down.

It escalated from there. I never tried to look for it or catch it, but it kept presenting itself. Once, he went on a family trip somewhere, and I couldn't join because I was working. He said he was going with his cousins and their wives. I later saw a picture in a tabloid of him with a girl sitting on his lap. It wasn't a clear picture, it was a bit blurry, but it was him. The girl, I wasn't so sure. The best part, when I showed it to him when he got back, was that he was mad at me for buying the magazine. He insisted it was just a fan who wanted a picture.

"She sat on your lap," I said. "She sat on your manhood to take a picture! That's just a little too much, don't you think?" I realized later that I knew the girl. She'd been at our house, and he had even tried to put her in one of the shows he tried to produce. It wasn't a random meeting. I really must have wanted a fairy tale at that point because I let it slide.

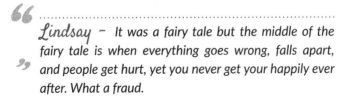

Lindsay – It was a fairy tale but the middle of the fairy tale is when everything goes wrong, falls apart, and people get hurt, yet you never get your happily ever after. What a fraud.

I even believed him once when I caught him sharing romantic texts and calls with a girl. He told me that her mom asked him to flirt with her to stop her from marrying a guy they didn't like. Imagine that? It was a very elaborate story and I believed it. I wanted to ask the girl if it was true, but how could I if it was a plan between him and her parents? Yes, yes, I was not thinking straight, or maybe not thinking at all.

Sometimes, even when you know that you have to leave, it's hard. And I think that's where I was. We had about two years invested in the relationship, and there were great days among the bad ones. One evening when I was home alone and waiting for him to come back from a trip the doorbell rang. When I opened the door I found a stack of photos on my front steps—my guy with various girls. It was all very Tiger Woods–like. There were hours, days, and weeks of fighting before we finally decided to mend things and try it again. At one point, his mom, who was a super sweet lady, said, "He's a good boy, he just needs time. He doesn't hit you, does he?" *Huh? Wait, say what?*

The final blow arrived when we were traveling together in Texas on his business trip. We were at the point where we were talking about marriage and the next step in our relationship. We were staying at a hotel. In the middle of the night, I don't know why, I woke up and went to the bathroom. He was charging his phone there. I stared at it as if to see if it would either say "Come on" or "Hands off." I naturally just thought that it had invited me to look at it. The phone basically called my name and said, "Hey, check me out."

So I looked through his texts and found a few that were definitely inappropriate for someone in a committed relationship. Texts like: *Baby, I can't wait to see you. I miss you.* That's what it finally took for me to stop and realize, *this is not for me.* Sitting there in that bathroom I asked myself, *do I want this for the rest of my life?* My answer was a definite no. *Stick a fork in me. I'm done.* It took me a while to come to the conclusion, but once I did, I knew there was no turning back. If I'm with someone, I want to be with him. And him with me. If he's not, then it's over.

While he was asleep, I quietly packed and left the room. I drove to the airport and got on the first flight back. There was no need to wake him up and have an argument. There was nothing he could have said that night that would have changed my mind. I knew he'd try, too, and I think I realized that night that I'd heard too many of his stories. I knew the truth in that moment. That's how we ended. Quietly, without a big production. I'm the kind of person who will exercise every single option before throwing in the towel. I tried. I rationalized. I wanted him to be different. I wanted him to be better. But he wasn't.

It took a long time, but I learned that perception is reality, and sometimes we are so occupied with getting close to a dream that we choose to believe the lies rather than the truth. But the truth always catches up. It always catches up. That night at the hotel it did. I later found out it wasn't just one girl, there were others. With women who had hung out at our house, been part of our circle. My advice to anyone who has that gut feeling or thinks her guy will change: He won't. A cheater never changes. A cheetah never changes its spots.

— The Over-Analyzation —

Karina

If another woman, or women, steals your man, there is no better revenge than letting her keep him. Real men can't be stolen.

Lindsay

These guys who are perpetual cheaters want to have their cake and eat it, too. I had a boyfriend who was the lead singer of a band and my first love. I trusted him with all of my heart and was absolutely devastated to learn that he had cheated on me throughout our multi-year relationship. The kicker was that I didn't find out about the cheating until *after* we broke up, while talking to a female friend of his who had been intimate with him during our relationship. Like Karina, I had been so in love and wanted to believe that he was better than he was that I got caught up in the idea of him. And that bag of condoms? Holding them for a friend? This guy screams "liar"! And that's the problem with cheaters—they're also liars. My mom always reminds me to watch out for the manipulators, that in less than ten minutes with most of us, a guy will know what we're all about, what we want to hear, and keep feeding us that BS to get what he wants. In this case, he ate all of Karina's cake and a bunch of other side pastries. No wonder he's been looking quite a bit fuller in the face.

Guy's Corner

Ralph

His excuses are weak. They're weak. He needs a good writer. The friend's box of condoms story, I love that. I love the fact that she believed him. Karina is a *benefit-of-the-doubt* girl. But there is that forgive me once, fool me once element to this. You can't fool me twice. As far as the story saying "they've asked me to flirt with her": Hey, listen, she bought the condom-carrying story, maybe she'll buy this one. That's what he was thinking. Hopefully she was out the door after that one.

Grooming Gone Wrong

I was on a date with a very fashion-forward man. I think the term that we are now accustomed to is "metrosexual." He was dressed as if he was about to do a casual shoot for *Jersey Shore Magazine* (if something like that even exists). His hair was slicked back with enough gel to last any other man at least a year; his shirt was unbuttoned enough to showcase his collarbone, which made me notice how he stayed in shape (by carrying a big chain around his neck); and he wore a hooded jacket that was a size too small for him, probably to enhance his muscles. His sleeves were rolled up, revealing a cluster of bracelets on his wrists. It was obvious he had given this outfit quite a bit of thought, and he was proud of it—and the helmet head. Add to that, he wore excessive amounts of cologne. Since we didn't really plan what we were going to do on the date, I opted for a cute summer dress, high heels (naturally), and my hair curled Farrah Fawcett style. Or at least I aimed for that look. We strolled the streets, figuring out what we wanted to do. The date was going great. I'm not a huge fan of people putting their arms around my neck or shoulders. I always wonder why they think that I would enjoy the proximity of their armpit to my shoulder. So usually I politely let them know that I'd much rather hold hands. Mr. Perfumania didn't get my hints right away, and he kept trying to put me in a headlock as we walked. Needless to say, it was bad enough it was one of my pet peeves, but his bracelets would catch my hair, and every time he moved his arm, he pulled my hair out. After about three or four of his attempts at grooming me with his bracelets, I started to see red. He found it very entertaining and funny. "I'm sorry! Hahaha. Are you okay? I feel like Vidal Sassoon. Hahaha," he said while laughing with his mouth wide open. I was seriously contemplating hitting him in the head with my purse, but then I realized that most likely there would be no damage since he had a freaking helmet on from gel and hairspray. So I did the next best thing. In one swift move, I reached for his hair, grabbed on tightly to a string of it, and pulled with all my strength. A sizable amount of his slicked back hair ended up in my hand, probably a little more than he had pulled out from my head with his bracelets. And to make things worse for him, the hair around the part that I grabbed stubbornly stood up in what looked like a crown of a rooster. Now, I couldn't stop laughing. Groom that, cock-a-doodle-do! —*Karina*

Lindsay and Karina

We love Cheryl, and we have all shared many dating stories with one another. She's witty, beautiful, and tons of fun. This one is hilarious.

Cheating Asshole Guy

Cheryl Burke, Professional Dancer, LA

It's fair to say I reached a level (high or low, I'm not sure) with a boyfriend who I knew was cheating on me. Years ago, before *Dancing with the Stars,* I was in a relationship with my then–dance partner. We'd met on the dance floor, obviously, and when you dance with someone, it intensifies the heat. The intimacy between two people happens faster than if they were just courting each other the old-fashioned way. We met and quickly fell for each other and then moved in together. We were living in New York at the time, in an apartment in Harlem.

Six months into it, I knew he was cheating. He wouldn't come home at night on time. Sometimes I'd smell perfume on him that wasn't mine. A bunch of little things led me to the conclusion he was stepping out. I admit, I went through his phone, and everything was deleted. That appeared to be a bad sign, too. There were a number of inappropriate things that added up to one thing in my mind. I had no proof and I couldn't point to one thing in particular, but I had women's intuition. It was just a feeling in my gut that this guy was messing around on me. I knew he wasn't being faithful.

Dancing with the Stars had contacted me to work for them, and when they originally offered, I told them only if my dance partner could join, too. They didn't want him; they only wanted me. During this period I had the feeling he was being sketchy, however, so when they called I said yes. I looked at it as a chance to sneak out of the relationship without much controversy and move myself to LA. I wasn't a big fan of confrontation. I figured that I would leave, he could cheat in peace, and eventually we'd just drift apart. It wouldn't

124

exactly be a clean break, but it would fizzle out. Surprisingly, when I told him I was going, he still wanted to stay together. He encouraged me to go but wanted to hold on to the relationship.

A few months in, he wanted to visit me in LA. I was training for my first season with the show, but I figured it would be fine. I was so bad at breaking up with people or firing anyone. I just wanted it to go away, but I didn't want to deal with it. As crazy as it sounds, I decided I'd get him to LA and, somehow, I'd catch him in the act. I wasn't exactly sure how that was going to happen, but I fantasized about it, hoping it would. It was my goal for the trip.

One night, we decided to go out and do some social dancing with my friends. We were in a club, and as we were all hanging out, I noticed this really hot girl come in and walk by. I saw him sort of gawk over in her direction, which was no surprise to me. I looked at them both and decided to set my plan into motion. It was the perfect moment.

I watched this girl walk across the club and then I made my move. I approached her and said, "I'm in a relationship I need to get out of. I know he's cheating, but I haven't really caught him and I haven't seen it. If I give you $100 and I go to the bathroom," I said, holding my hands up to make air quotes, "will you make out with my boyfriend for me? So I can finally catch him?"

"Fuck yeah," she said. "I'm all over it."

It's fair to say I surprised even myself. I'd never done anything like that before, but I was desperate to get out of this thing. I needed to see this guy cheat with my own eyes. Then I could just walk away and leave it alone with no stress. I just wanted to know. I could then say with confidence, "Fuck you. I knew you were cheating this whole time."

I paid my partner in crime $100 and walked back over to my boyfriend. I got him up on the dance floor but then said, "I need to go to the bathroom." I left him there in the middle of the dance floor and then went and hid behind a palm tree to watch.

He never saw it coming. Not five minutes later, she walked up to him and they were grinding away at each other. They were basically fuck-dancing. It was perfect. He didn't even pretend to resist. She went in for a kiss and then bam, they were fully making out. It was so easy, it was pathetic. I came out from behind my palm tree and walked up to him and said, "I knew you were cheating on me." I went crazy on him. It couldn't have worked out better. There we were in the middle of this club and I made a huge scene, going so far as to slap him in the face. It was all very dramatic. It was amusing, too. I really laid it on pretty thick. The best part, even after watching it all unfold, was that the guy denied it. Like every other guy would.

> 66 ....
> *Lindsay* − This is classic. Love it! He didn't know who he was messing with. And what an idiot. What kind of action did he think he was going to get while she was in the bathroom? Then to deny it? The joke is on him! Bravo, Cheryl.
> ....

> 66 ....
> *Karina* − Amazing. This might be my favorite "screw you, loser" story ever. People who cheat are usually very insecure. He got what he deserved. Tap out! And as for the $100, it was the best investment ever!
> ....

Looking back, if he had been the perfect guy, I wouldn't have had to go to such extreme lengths. If I hadn't gotten the call from *Dancing with the Stars,* I might have still been living in New York with him. I learned a lot. When a guy is controlling and overprotective, that's a bad sign that he might be up to something because he thinks you are. When he lies about how soon he'll be home and then takes hours, that's not okay either. That's a sign something's going on. Warning to girls out there: When his phone is always off, it's not good. And while I truly don't suggest this is the best way to go, it helped me to go through his phone. I didn't uncover anything, but he was very clearly a compulsive deleter and that said something to me.

I don't know whatever happened to the girl at the bar, but I can say with certainty it was $100 well spent. I've never done anything like it again, but I have stayed away from the bad boys from that moment on. I learned my lesson the hard way. And in some small way, I feel like spending that $100 paved the way for me to meet my current boyfriend, who is a trustworthy, loyal, solid guy.

Chapter 7:
The Jealous Tyrant

Controlling Guy

Karina

Sometimes it seems like lying is the better solution. But it never is. Never.

I was dating a guy who thought I was exotic. He was from the Midwest, so I thought he was exotic, too. We dated for about a year, then we started living together. He was a professional athlete, so he traveled a lot. I started to notice that he was very territorial, especially when he was away. For that reason, I got in trouble with him a lot. He was very much of the opinion: "She's mine. I want her now, here." That's how he viewed me.

Frequently, while he was away, I'd have to tell him, "Baby, I'm heading straight home and going to sleep." He always wanted a call from me when I was in bed.

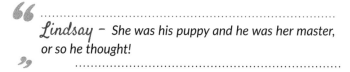

"

Lindsay – She was his puppy and he was her master, or so he thought!

"

Occasionally, I'd call him from wherever I was. I'd find a quiet place while I was out with my friends and pretend I was home in bed. I wasn't doing anything wrong. I wanted to go out. One night after the show, Lindsay and I headed into a club. I wanted to let my hair down and have fun, which was usually the case post show. Instead of getting into a big fight about it, I decided to lie. I dragged Lindsay into a stall in the bathroom at the club.

"I'm going call him. Tell him I'm home. Then we can go have fun," I said.

There's nowhere very quiet in the club, of course, with music and sound effects in the background. But the bathroom seemed good enough. I knew I had to be quick so if the door opened, the noise wouldn't blast in.

I dialed. "Yeah, baby, I'm so tired, it's been like the longest day. I've been up for like fourteen hours. I'm going straight to bed."

Automatic flushing toilets never work. I don't know who invented them, but they never flush when you need them to. Apparently, they flush when you don't need them to.

In the middle of my "I'm already in bed": *Swooooosh*. The toilet flushed on me. I almost died.

"Are you in the bathroom?"

"Yeah, sorry. You caught me. I didn't want to tell you I was in the bathroom."

"Why not?" he asked.

"Well, you know. It's a little embarrassing," I said.

This wasn't working out as planned, but finally he told me to call him in the morning. We did the "I love you's" and hung up.

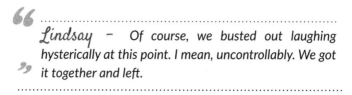

Lindsay – *Of course, we busted out laughing hysterically at this point. I mean, uncontrollably. We got it together and left.*

At the end of the night, we decided it would be best to avoid the paparazzi by coming out of the back of the club. We wouldn't get caught. I orchestrated an elaborate escape through the back door, and just as we walked out, wouldn't you know it: There was a huge crowd of cameras.

"Oh, crap," I said. We weaved in and out, trying not to get caught.

We got to the car. "I think we made it. We're good. Nobody took a picture of us. I'm sure of it," I said.

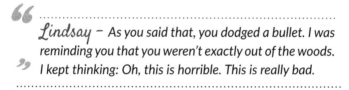

Lindsay – *As you said that, you dodged a bullet. I was reminding you that you weren't exactly out of the woods. I kept thinking: Oh, this is horrible. This is really bad.*

The next morning I woke up when he called.

"So, you were in bed when we spoke last night?"

"I was," I said. "Yeah." I wondered if I'd made the news.

"Well, I'm looking at a picture of you coming out of a club last night."

"Oh, yeah. I stopped by quickly, yeah," I said. "I knew you would be upset."

We settled it, but this was a year into a relationship. It was tough to be that watched and controlled. I guess my free-spirited clubbing was too much for him because he decided to do something about it.

Later that week, Lindsay told me I had a meeting with a Twitter executive at a restaurant in Malibu. They wanted to talk about monetizing my account.

❝

Lindsay – It is nearly impossible to get Karina anywhere
unless it has to do with work. Especially during the show,
never mind on the night of the show. Never mind getting
her to Malibu. The Twitter story was a setup.

My Twitter account? Okay. I wasn't sure what that even meant, but I agreed to it, even though it wasn't like I had six million followers or something. Lindsay told me the president of Twitter thought I had a lot of value. Umm, sure. Whatever you say.

I was leaving from work, and I'd just done a costume dance from the future, so I had feathers in my hair and almost a Mohawk. And black lipstick. I wore a skimpy black dress. I looked like I was going to some super crazy Halloween party.

Lindsay met me in the limo after the show.

"Can I go dressed like this?" I asked.

"Yeah, let's just go. We've got to get to Malibu."

"I look like Elvira."

"Don't worry about it," she said. "Let's just get moving."

We walked into Gladstones and it was oddly empty. It was lit beautifully with candles. We were right on the water. Lindsay kept looking at her phone, and as soon as we sat down, she got up and said she had to take a call.

"Where are you going? Come back. I don't know what he looks like. Don't leave me!" I pleaded.

She walked away and I was worried. I was alone and didn't know what the president of Twitter even looked like, but since no one was there I figured he'd find me.

I looked up and saw someone come in. It wasn't the Twitter guy. It was my guy.

Is he following me? This is ridiculous. I was not happy. I knew he was controlling, but he knew I had a business meeting. I told him I couldn't take him with me because it was business, and yet he showed up anyway. I was angry. As got closer to me, I realized he was in a suit—dressed to the nines. That was strange. Then I realized he had tears in his eyes. I figured something was up and then wondered if something had happened to his parents or mine or something.

He got down on one knee and took out a box. I said, "Holy shit!" Out loud. He opened it, and inside was a beautiful ring.

"Will you marry me?" he asked.

My response: "Am I not meeting the president of Twitter?"

> **Lindsay** – I would like to point out that I had suggested to this guy that he wait just a few weeks until the season of Karina's show ended and things settled down. I had also suggested a helicopter to a table with champagne at a really cool place. Not . . . Gladstones.

I was so crazy. I said yes, even though I asked to keep it on the DL until the season was over, because I thought that was the more professional thing to do.

— The Over-Analyzation —

Karina

In the end, we were two different people. He hunted animals. I was an animal lover and an advocate. I cried every time he killed Bambi. I wanted a family and a career, and he wanted to move away to a small, quiet town. In many ways, we were polar opposites, too. So it just wasn't going to work.

Lindsay

I thought that she would marry this guy. I actually really did. But I knew that the engagement was not going to be what she wanted. I just knew. So I knew it was the wrong night, it was the wrong time, it was the wrong location, it was all wrong. Yet that's what he wanted to do. So that's what it was. Add to that he was super controlling. I mean even with the engagement, he only wanted to listen to what he wanted. Even though I'm Karina's best friend and know what she would have liked because of course, as girlfriends do, we had talked about the timing of an engagement plus what each of us would find super romantic. On top of that she's a free spirit, which never would have worked with Mr. Controlling.

Guy's Corner

Jacoby

No, no, no. Karina can't be with a controlling guy. That was never going to work.

Ricardo

These guys ask Karina to marry them far too soon. She's too fabulous for words and they want to tie her down, but Karina is not a woman to be tied down by a man ever. If anyone is going to have Karina for life, he's the one who gives her the longest leash ever. That's the one who's going to have Karina.

Lindsay and Karina

Lesley and Lindsay have been friends since third grade. Lesley is a genuinely good person, beautiful inside and out, yet like us she still hasn't met "the one." She understands that dating is a numbers game, and for every dozen bad dates, there's always that gem. Laughing about the disasters is easier when you have girlfriends in the same boat as you and also when you have faith that at some point, the right guy is going to walk into your life and suddenly all the previous disappointments will have been worth it. Not to mention, contrary to some women in LA, we do eat: We definitely don't want any man telling us when and how much food he deems appropriate.

Girls-Don't-Eat Guy

Lesley, Fashion and Beauty Marketing Consultant, Hollywood

Everyone in this town is like Peter Pan, so when I came across a guy online who had actually been married, had a kid, and sort of done it once already, I thought, *maybe this is worth pursuing.* I figured he was likely more grounded than a lot of the lifelong bachelors. We exchanged a few e-mails and spoke on the phone, and while he seemed slightly awkward, I chalked it up to being nervous.

We arranged to meet and he chose a restaurant. He seemed excited by his pick and told me there were celebrities there, so that would be great. I explained that that kind of thing didn't matter to me at all, that I was just looking for good food and good company. He insisted this was the place to go, that it was a "very cool spot."

When I pulled up, I was slightly worried I had arrived at the wrong place. He'd made such a big deal about where we were going, but, in fact, this place was nothing more than a little Chinese restaurant, like the one that's down everyone's street. I figured at least the food would be good, though it certainly wasn't first-date material. The restaurant was bright and uncomfortable and a little strange. It did not in any way match the way he'd described it when he played it up like it was the best. Still, I was a good sport and sat down.

"Tell me a few things that look good to you and I'll select from there," he said.

"I mostly eat seafood," I said. I scanned the menu and said I would be good with any of the three shrimp dishes and listed off a few veggie dishes that looked good as well. I pointed out a few other things that also looked good. I gave him lots of choices.

"None of that really looks good to me." He proceeded to list some beef dishes he liked instead.

As politely as I could, I said those wouldn't really be my picks.

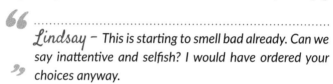

Lindsay – This is starting to smell bad already. Can we say inattentive and selfish? I would have ordered your choices anyway.

I was a little stunned, but I assumed he'd figure it out and we could each at least have a dish we both liked. The waitress came over to us to take our order. She explained how many dishes people usually order—a couple of entrées and some sides usually being enough. This guy then proceeded to order one beef dish and one side dish. Nothing I liked. It was everything I had pointed out I didn't like and half the amount of food the waitress had suggested.

Without commenting on the choice of food, I pointed out the amount.

"Do you think that's going to be enough? Maybe we should order one more thing?" I asked, hoping to get a little shrimp in there.

"Oh, that's fine," he said. "Girls don't need to eat a lot."

"What's that?" I asked.

"Girls don't need to eat a lot."

"I thought that's what you said," I said.

I decided not to say anything or attempt to order anything else. In my head I knew we were done. This wasn't going to go anywhere from here. I turned to the waitress, still there hearing all of this but not reacting, and said, "I'll have a glass of wine." I looked down at the menu.

He jumped in and said, "Red or white?"

I said, "Red."

He proceeded to choose the glass for me and ordered it.

There are times that I don't mind guys taking the initiative, but this didn't feel like it was coming from a nice place. It felt more like a weird and controlling thing.

> 66
> *Karina* – Who the hell does he think he is? Does he think she doesn't have a mind of her own? Or is this a money thing? Maybe he only had enough money to buy the one entrée and wanted to make sure she got the cheapest glass of wine possible. He was clearly trying to limit the order. Was he hoping to eat in front of her as she watched?

> 66
> *Lindsay* – I would have come down with a severe stomachache. How rude.

As I sipped my wine, I decided I would just go home after and pick something up along the way. I knew I could meet up with a friend or whatever. I just wanted the date to end, for him to eat his stupid beef, and to be done with it.

As we waited for the small bits of food to arrive, I said, "So tell me about your son."

"Well, I met a girl online. We fell really hard for each other. Within a week or two, we started trying to have a baby."

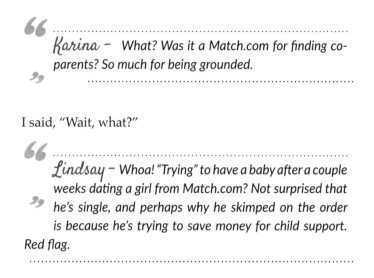

Karina – *What? Was it a Match.com for finding co-parents? So much for being grounded.*

I said, "Wait, what?"

Lindsay – *Whoa! "Trying" to have a baby after a couple weeks dating a girl from Match.com? Not surprised that he's single, and perhaps why he skimped on the order is because he's trying to save money for child support. Red flag.*

Not only was I thinking, *Red flag* but also the entire building was turning red around me, flashing red. This was not my kind of guy.

"So, you decided to have a baby with someone you just met?" I asked.

"Yes. Fortunately, before the baby was born, we realized that we weren't really meant to be."

I was thinking, *yeah, that's the kind of conversation I'm sure pregnant women love to have.* Fortunately the food arrived and was a distraction from the awkwardness of the conversation. I didn't know what else to say to the baby mama situation, and I just wanted to get out of the restaurant at that point.

Once the plates were on the table, he said, "I'll serve you." He scooped a little bit of rice into a tiny bowl and scooped everything else out onto his plate. He gave me about one quarter of the rice and took the rest for himself. I'd never had anyone do that before.

"Gee, what if I'm hungry?" I asked.

"You are a girl. You don't need that much food," he said.

The waitress came over and asked if I'd like anything else and he jumped in and said, "No, she's good."

> *Lindsay* – Wow, this guy has some weird hang-up. He shouldn't have asked you to dinner had he not wanted you to eat.

> *Karina* – Can someone please slap this guy? I'm not a mean person, but at this point I'm hoping he will choke on that beef. Meathead.

If that wasn't enough, he just continued to get weirder. He went on to say how his kid was cute and the joy in his life, but that it had obviously been a bad life decision. He said it was difficult because all of his friends were married and had families. He said that since he didn't have a wife, he had no one to hang out with.

> *Karina* – Maybe if he didn't ration food, he'd have more friends or even a wife. And at the rate he was going, his wife would die of starvation.

"Hang out with your married friends," I said. "I do it all the time."

He said no, that wasn't what he wanted to do.

"Well, you're thirty-nine. Your friends will be coupled up by now. I don't know what else to tell you."

Then he dropped another beauty. "Well, I'm excited that a good friend of mine is getting a divorce. So I'll have my boy back to hang with."

He went on to tell me his only single friend was kind of a loser, over forty, and still living at home. That is, when he wasn't in jail.

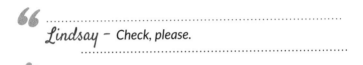

Lindsay – *Check, please.*

At this point I was beginning to think that perhaps I was on *Candid Camera*. I started looking around to see if anyone was recording this date. There was nothing normal about this guy, but none of it had made itself apparent in his profile. After the food had been cleared, and I was clearly itching to get out, he said, "You don't really seem like you're having a great time."

"No, it's fine. You win some, you lose some," I said. "I really just don't think this is a great love connection."

"I'm sorry if I upset you," he said.

"You didn't upset me at all," I said. "Just some of the things, like your manners, are a little bit different than what I'm used to. No big deal at all. Nothing to get upset about."

We made our way outside and he said, "So, do you want me to come over? I'm really good at full-body massage."

I looked at him and said, "What?"

"I'm really good at giving massages," he repeated without irony.

"Even after I told you that I don't feel anything for you?" I asked. *No. I don't want you to come over and touch my naked body.* "No, thank you."

I got in my car, said good-bye, and left. I was gone from my house for one hour start to finish. Fortunately, he didn't try to contact me again.

Chapter 8:
At Least Pretend You Care, Guy

I-Look-Better-On-Paper Guy

Lindsay

A year and a half after a difficult and emotionally draining breakup with the father of my son, I decided to start dating again. I'd done a bit of dating, but not a lot. I'd tried some online dating to get my feet wet and was finally starting to feel open to trying it again. One evening, Karina, Melissa, and I were at a movie premiere—one of the Spiderman movies. I was waiting for Karina and Melissa to finish on the red carpet when I spotted a guy looking at me. I was sort of looking back—he was cute in an interesting way. He was with someone, but it didn't seem like they were together romantically. Since Melissa knew everybody, I said, "Get us over there to talk to him. He's looking at me."

So she did. And eventually we were all talking. The conversation was light, but I made clear I knew who he was and that I was a fan of his show. "It's one of my guilty pleasures," I said, trying to flirt. We had some common interests, too. He told me he was a single dad. I wasn't certain, but it seemed like there was chemistry between us.

The girl he was with tugged on his sleeve and said, "We've got to go." As he was saying good-bye, I am not sure what came over me, but I dropped my card into his pocket. He asked me if I'd ever want to go on his show.

"I don't want to be on TV, but I'd love to talk off camera," I said.

I didn't hear from him. Six or so months later, Karina and I were at another event. We bumped into the guy and both realized we recognized each other.

"I know you!" he said. "I don't know how, though."

"Oh, we've met." I started teasing him a bit but wouldn't tell him where or when.

At one point, he pulled me aside and said, "Seriously, do you feel this?" I said yes, I did. Then he said to Karina and some others within our circle, "This is what chemistry looks like."

> 66
> *Karina* – Great pickup line. Wish he had a better memory, though.
> 99

"Don't you remember where we met?" I asked.

"I'm so bad. I don't."

I filled him in. Then he told me the girl he was with saw me put the card in his pocket and was so jealous she took it!

"I went to look for it when I got home because I wanted to call you—I thought you were super cute. And it wasn't there."

After a couple of weeks of texting and calling, we went out on a date. He took me to Picca, my favorite restaurant. We had an amazing time filled with great conversation. He told me he admired that I was a strong woman and that his mom was also a strong woman.

> 66
> *Karina* – Uh-oh. You remind him of his mom. Again, either he has mastered the skill of picking up or this was just good the second time around.
> 99

And then we made out like teenagers in his car. It was the craziest chemistry.

After dinner we went to this bar called High in Venice. It's a rooftop bar with fire pits, couches, and blankets. It was amazing—overlooking the water that surrounds you. We made out the entire time. At one point, I had to go downstairs to use the bathroom and he threw me up against the wall in the stairwell and kissed me. I loved it. It was amazing.

It was a busy time, so after the first date, we both had difficulty squeezing in the scheduling of dates, so we would kind of sneak time to see each other. We would literally just chitchat and then make out in his car—after work, before he had to go take care of his kids, and in between me taking care of mine. It was fun. The downside, like with many guys, was he was all about him. He was very down on his ex and seemed to take no responsibility for the breakdown of his marriage. He was intrigued by our chemistry and we had a connection, but there was something holding him back, too.

> 66
> *Karina* – *Those are called "warning signs," and you were ignoring them. Well, you were seeing them. We talked about them. But you were making excuses for them. Which we've all done. Convenient, easy, and yet somewhat resistant. At this point, put the sensors on but keep an open mind. Or treat him the way he was begging to be treated: as a booty call on your terms.*

The booty call thing isn't exactly my style. During Emmy weekend, he was going to be at a hotel downtown. He invited me to come and hang out there. We hadn't had sex together. I'd told him my position on sex, too—we had a conversation about it, and he seemed to respect the fact that I wasn't a girl who slept around. I definitely wasn't ready for it with him since we weren't in a monogamous relationship, but I agreed to drive downtown and see him anyway.

He answered the door in his boxer briefs which caught me by surprise, but he was cute. We made out a bit that night. It was fun, but I still wasn't ready to proceed and definitely not under the circumstances.

> 66
> *Karina* – *Maybe answering in his underwear was a test, to see if you could resist sex?*

Here's the thing: I've had a lot of sex in my day. I have. But after having my son, I decided I wanted to be in a committed and monogamous relationship and not be sleeping around. I'm not judging—I'm all for other people doing it. It just wasn't for me at that stage of my life, despite the chemistry between us. Once sex is in play, the stakes get too high, and sometimes I stay with someone too long for the wrong reason. With that, he kissed me good-bye and told me that he was traveling for a while but he'd call me when he was back in town.

He was cute. I was interested and intrigued,. We got along so well, too. But I didn't hear much from him after that night. He disappeared. No calls. No texts. Nothing.

> 66
> *Karina* – Did he think you were going to jump on him in his boxer briefs? You were upset, but you did handle it
> 99
> well, I thought.

He basically disappeared. I was bummed, but I moved on. That was in April.

Around Thanksgiving, I sent out a mass text to everyone in my contact file wishing them a happy holiday. Surprisingly, he texted me back a string of texts.

Hey stranger, how are you?

I've been thinking so much about you.

I wanted to reconnect.

Can we talk sometime?

I'm sorry I disappeared.

I agreed to talk. He told me he was on a cruise with his kids and he'd call when he got back. I wasn't interested in dating him anymore. I was curious to see if he had an excuse.

A couple of weeks later, I was listening to my voice mail messages in the car. There was one from him. I wasn't sure how I'd missed it or when it came in—before or after the text exchange. I called him back right away and we got into it a little bit.

He apologized profusely.

"I'm sorry for disappearing."

"Yeah, listen," I said, "that was really rude. Whether or not you wanted to date, you should have absolutely had the decency to let me know that you weren't interested."

"Let me tell you what was going on," he said. "The way that I felt when I was with you was unlike anything I had ever felt before. I was married to my high school sweetheart for fifteen years. The fact that I had never felt that way and all of a sudden felt this way for someone I barely knew, I started to think, well, maybe it's just that—maybe I was doing something wrong with her. So I went back to her. To see what had happened and what I did wrong."

"Did it work out?" I asked. I felt like at that point I could have been happy for him. An amazing thing would have come from our exchange.

"I went back and I didn't feel it. I tried and I tried," he said. "I figured since it had been so easy with you, someone I barely knew, maybe it could work with her. But it didn't. We realized the divorce was inevitable."

I felt so badly for him. He told me he didn't stop thinking about me. I respected his attempt to get back with his wife. I thought it spoke to his character and was an admirable quality.

"I know you probably don't want to see me, but I'd like to just see you and grab a drink, talk, whatever."

> *Karina* – *Puuhhleeeassse. Come on. That's like the oldest trick in the book. "I'm sorry, you are amazing, but I had a duty to figure out if what I had with my ex could still be there." Whatever. He should have at least shot you a text to let you know what was happening. This guy should have watched a romantic comedy to see how it worked or he should have taken his B.S. elsewhere.*

"That's fine," I said. "We can definitely talk."

We ended up agreeing to meet at a place called Toscanova for drinks. That night, before we met, I was in a business meeting with a matchmaker involved with a new TV show. I asked her to stick around and keep an eye on our meeting and to assess. She agreed.

He arrived and the heat was there again. He told me I looked great and we sat and talked for a long time. He asked that we at least try to be friends, and if something came of it, great. Afterward, the matchmaker told me he was totally into me. She could tell by his body language and the fact that he couldn't keep his eyes off of me, that he was zeroed in on only me the entire time. She even said, "I wouldn't be surprised if this is the guy you're supposed to be with." That made me want to give him another chance.

> *Karina* – *I'm sorry, but no, no, no. The whole thing screamed scam. He was back in town and wanted to feel alive and desired. As much as I respect the matchmaker's opinion, this guy would need to jump through hoops to prove that he's not scamming. Leaving someone hanging is total high school. Not when you are forty and have children. Aretha Franklin said it best: "R.E.S.P.E.C.T."*

Some time passed because I was traveling with Karina. He said when I got back, he wanted to have me over, cook dinner for me, and that we could just talk and have wine and relax. The nice thing was that it wasn't just physical between us. We had an intellectual connection, too. The lack of self-awareness had re-emerged, though— he still fully blamed his ex for everything, and hearing him complain like that wasn't attractive. We eventually made out like we had in the past and rolled around wrestling on the living room floor. It was hot, but I left at midnight. There wasn't going to be sex as a reward for his disappearing act. Ultimately, it was a great night—incredible, in fact. I had a great time with him and wondered as I drove home if it was meant to be and timing had just gotten in the way.

He texted me the next day.

Miss you. Can't wait to see you again. Then he called that night after work.

"Are you missing something?" he asked.

"What do you mean?"

"Your earrings. I think I almost swallowed them."

I realized my earrings, my favorite earrings, must have fallen out at his place.

"One was under the coffee table and the other was in the seat cushion of the couch," he said.

"I'm so glad you found them!"

We figured out that our schedules were crazy for the weeks that followed, so he would send them to me. My assumption was that he would messenger them. Instead, when I got back from my trip, there was a regular envelope—like a plain white $1 envelope—in my mailbox. The bottom corner had been ripped open. I looked inside. There were no earrings, but there was a pink Post-it note.

"I believe these belong to your ears!" The earrings had been stolen. I texted him.

Oh my gosh your letter came but my earrings didn't make it.

Those were my favorite earrings.

I'm bummed.

They were stolen in transit.

His response:

Wow, that's crazy.

I didn't follow up. I fully expected flowers, or an attempt to make up for my loss with a new pair of earrings. Or something. But I got nothing. So I said nothing. The next time I heard from him was with an invite to the launch of a product line he was endorsing. It was an idea I had given him while we were dating the first time around.

I responded with a text.

I see you took my advice!

He texted me back.

I always take the advice of a smart woman.

> **""**
> *Karina* – Was he Veruca Salt from Willy Wonka & the Chocolate Factory? "Me, me me! I want it now! I want the whole world!" Urgh! No good deed goes unpunished.
> **""**

And that was it.

— The Over-Analyzation —

Lindsay

You lost my earrings. You couldn't care less. You stole my idea, didn't thank me, just invited me to your launch party. You disappeared and came back after I sent a mass text out. At what point did I need to be smacked over the head to be told that this guy was a selfish A-hole?

Karina

"Selfishness is not living as one wishes to live; it is asking others to live as one wishes to live." —Oscar Wilde

This guy was rude, inconsiderate, and totally self-absorbed. He wanted a rebound relationship. He should have at least been upfront about that fact. You gave him a lot of chances. I get it. He was apologetic, and the attempt with his wife seemed positive and admirable. But he was lonely and totally not ready for a relationship. You were completely the wrong type of girl to fill the void of loneliness but not get involved with him.

Guy's Corner

Ricardo

The earrings are unforgivable. He should have handled with care since he knew Lindsay cared. As for the boxers, what was he packing in there? We all want to know!

Jacoby

I would have used the earrings as an excuse to get another date with Lindsay. I would have held on to them and told her I'd give them to her on our next date. The fact that he did nothing to fix losing them—that's not cool either. He's not too smart is my guess. Not street smart, anyway. He should have known somebody would take the earrings. He should have replaced them after they were gone. He should be working overtime to make up for that.

Lindsay and Karina

I remember when we first heard this story. It was almost impossible to believe someone could be so terrible to her.

I-Don't-Want-to-Go-Out-with-You-Even-Though-I-Asked Guy

Maya, Country Recording Artist, LA

Through mutual friends, I met a really great guy—or so I thought. At the time, I was newly single and I hadn't been on a date with a new person in a long time—maybe even a few years. He seemed really interested in me. He said he was going to pick me up. I agreed, but I gave him a friend's address instead of my own, because I didn't know him well enough to even let him know where I was living. I went to her place, and I worked hard to look great. I bought a new outfit and had my nails done so they'd pop. I wanted to look good.

He and I had arranged for an eight o'clock pickup. I was ready early of course and had spent some time getting dressed and made up. Fifteen minutes went by without a word, then thirty. I decided I should text him. It was a strange exchange.

Me: Are you almost here?

Him: Are we still on for dinner?

Me: Yes, are you coming to pick me up?

Him: Yeah. Sorry. I just had some chicken in the oven for poker night so I was waiting for that to cook.

A bunch of things went through my head at this point. I thought perhaps he was making dinner for me. I wondered if he was overwhelmed. I wondered if he burned his first attempt at chicken and had to make a second chicken and do the whole thing over again.

Karina – *I love that this stuff goes through a girl's head when in reality this guy is just being a dope. How come women are so good at making excuses for men? He forgot? And then he couldn't even come up with a better excuse to cover his tracks?*

Lindsay – *She's giving a guy she barely knows too much credit. We all do it, but when it comes to our girlfriends, we can see it right away. What's wrong with us?*

Me: *Would it be better if I just met you at your house? Or will you still come get me?*

To be clear: It was 8:45 at this point. He was forty-five minutes late and still no resolution. I was becoming really annoyed.

Him: *I would love to go to dinner with you tonight but I forgot I had poker night tonight.*

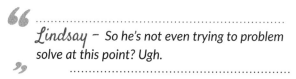

Lindsay – *So he's not even trying to problem solve at this point? Ugh.*

It felt like he was sort of freaking out at that point. But then I received a weird and confused text seconds later.

Him: *What's up for dinner?*

> 66
>
> *Karina* – *This guy can't make a decision. He might be drunk or delusional. If that were me, my answer would be: "A psychiatrist!"*
>
> 99

It was obvious that he'd mixed up the dates and just forgotten we had a plan, because by 9:00 p.m. we had no plan, he wasn't coming to pick me up, and he clearly had poker night happening. I put an end to the texting and dialed his number and simply said that he shouldn't worry about it, let's just bag it and do it another night. Not that I would go out with him again. But I wanted to be polite and just get out of the situation.

For weeks after that night he called me. He wanted to try to get together again. Despite the debacle, I was intrigued by him, but I knew I wouldn't have any respect for myself if I went out with him.

> 66
>
> *Karina* – *Go, girl! What he did was totally inappropriate and rude. He might have been a bigger star in his own mind. It's like a game of poker here: No one wants to quit when they're losing, and no one wants to quit easily when they are winning. I guess he thought the ball was in his court and now it was your turn to fix that.*
>
> 99

> 66
>
> *Lindsay* – *Why do we all give guys so many chances? Didn't Mama always say when a guy shows you who he is, believe him?*
>
> 99

A month or so after the night that never was, we figured out we were both going to the same party. We had mutual friends, so it was inevitable our paths would cross at some point. He offered to drive me. He had sort of grown on me, and with the exception of the first night, he had been nice on the phone in his million attempts to have a do-over. I agreed to go to the party with him. In my mind, all had been forgiven, and being friends wasn't such a bad thing. I was open to giving him another chance to be more than friends, but I wanted to be cautious.

We went to the party and had a nice time. We left together, and as we were headed back, we decided to make a stop at a birthday party for a friend of his. I didn't know anyone. I realized after not very long that he had left the party. He stranded me. Tears welled up in my eyes and it took all my strength not to cry. I felt so humiliated. I started talking to a guy who was there. He was being nice and could probably tell I was a little upset. My mood changed quickly when I realized I'd hit it off with this guy. Next thing I knew, he and I, along with some friends, left the party to go to another party at a nearby bar. Guy number one was at the second party, though, and when he saw me with guy number two, he walked up to me and told me he was angry with me. He told me his feelings were hurt, and he couldn't believe it. Yada, yada, yada. Still, I stayed and hung out with guy number two.

I felt guilty. I wasn't sure what the right thing to do was, and when guy number one left in a huff, I felt bad. I didn't know what exactly was going on, but the night felt like a mess. Suddenly, I was panicked. I had left my bag in guy number one's car. I had planned to change, and my makeup and everything was in there. Guy number two and I left the bar and grabbed a cab. He thought he was about to get lucky and score with me that night, but instead I had him drop me off at guy number one's apartment. I knew where he lived.

66

Karina - *Not by choice. She needed her stuff. Guy number two is still possibly a great guy. Can't blame him for hoping to get lucky.*

99

In that short period of time, I'd kind of fallen for guy number two. I felt emotional about leaving him and upset about chasing guy number one and getting yelled at. So while I would have liked to have just hung out with number two, I'd had too many hurt feelings that night and the situation was all too weird, so I just called it and went to grab my stuff. I went to number one's door and knocked, but no one answered. I knocked a few more times, and eventually he came to the door. There was another girl there that he was clearly with. He moved quickly.

He opened the door, not happy to have been interrupted, and asked me what I was doing there.

"I need to get my bag," I said. "I left it in your car."

Maybe for the girl's benefit, maybe for mine, he said, "I told you that it wasn't going to work out for us. I'm just not interested in you like that. I just like you as a friend."

"I'm only here to get my bag; I left it in the car. But thank you for humiliating me in front of everyone."

"Go outside," he said. "I'll bring you your bag."

"Well, do you mind if I wait inside while I wait for a cab? I have to call one. I don't know where I am."

"Absolutely not," he said. "Please just leave."

I did as ordered. I left and stood there on the corner, not even knowing where exactly I was, until he came down with my bag. As if it wasn't all humiliating enough, he, the girl he was rocking, and some friends all walked by when he dropped off my bag and continued on with their evening, leaving me there like a loser on the corner without saying a word.

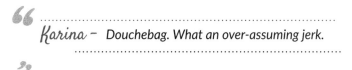

Karina – Douchebag. What an over-assuming jerk.

I decided I'd better call a cab. I dug my phone out of my bag and, of course, my phone was dead. I was standing in the middle of wherever with no ride home and no idea where I was going and no phone. Luckily, I was able to flag a cab that eventually came by. I figured out that I had a friend nearby as we drove away, so I went there. Home was too far and would have been too expensive of a cab ride.

It was the biggest nightmare of a date ever. Nothing could have been worse. But something great came of it. Guy number two took the time to get my number from someone else that night. He called me the next day and we've been dating ever since. It's been a year. And the sweet revenge of it all is that guy number one knows we're together. I ran into him once or twice and thanked him for being so awful. I said if he hadn't been, I'd never have met a truly great guy.

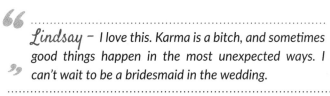

Lindsay – I love this. Karma is a bitch, and sometimes good things happen in the most unexpected ways. I can't wait to be a bridesmaid in the wedding.

Lessons That We Never Stop Learning

Don't make excuses for him (we all do it at one point or another, as you are learning as you read).

. . . .

Make sure you're not always available. Have a life of your own!

. . . .

Maintain a certain amount of mystery. Karina's ex still thinks she goes *number two* once a week, if that.

. . . .

Call the shots, but let him buy them.

. . . .

Don't sleep with him on the first date!

. . . .

Don't try to be what he wants you to be; be who you are.

. . . .

Look for someone who makes you better, not worse.

. . . .

If you don't respect him, the relationship won't last.

. . . .

If you don't trust him, the relationship won't last.

. . . .

Never stay with a guy who puts you down.

. . . .

If the guy has potential, give him three chances; by the third date you will either start to see more good qualities or perhaps more negative ones.

. . . .

Ask him questions and actually listen to the answers.

. . . .

Chapter 9:
Either He Can't Talk or He Can't Stop Talking (about Himself)

A Sweet Proposal

Karina

Like many other girls out there, I have met guys while I was at work. Just because my work is broadcast on national television doesn't make my dating experience that much different from yours. Sure, sometimes the guys are famous, sometimes not. But fame should not define a man. At the end of the day our experiences as girls trying to find *the one* are universal.

There is a well-known rumor that dancers make great lovers. Well, I guess it is all very subjective. Another dancer and I were friendly for years, but I wouldn't say we were friends. We didn't hang out after work, but we saw each other at work every day. We were cordial and nice to each other and, like everyone, we shared the occasional laugh. Eventually, it became clear he was trying to court me. I started to notice he would wait for me after my rehearsal so he could walk me to my car. Or he'd show up and give me a cupcake for no reason. He began revealing himself to be sweet, cute, and charming—the total opposite of his persona on TV. Out of nowhere, I thought, *what is going on? Is he pursuing me?*

One evening at the end of rehearsal, he was hanging out. He approached me and out of the blue, he said, "Why don't we date?"

"First of all, in the past you dated one of my friends, and I'm pretty certain she might still be in love with you. Second, you've had flings with multiple girls in that circle that I know and I have heard about it in detail." I had heard from many of them who went away or out with him and came back saying, "I totally did him in the bathroom." There were tons of hookups with random girls in random places.

"Let's date," he insisted.

"Absolutely not. Even though you dated my friend some years ago, there is still girl code. Well, at least I believe in it."

"It's been five or six years. It's long over and she's in love and is about to get married." I knew she was dating a guy she was crazy about. But old love sometimes dies super slow. To make things worse, I also knew she took full credit for educating this guy in the bedroom department. She said she had taken the time to teach him a lot of stuff. I never said it out loud, but I wondered, *how bad was he?*

"It's too weird. I've known you forever."

"It's not weird," he insisted.

"Get her permission and blessing, and I'll consider it. If what you're saying is true, it shouldn't be difficult."

Oddly, he did it, and she agreed.

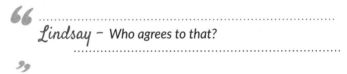

Lindsay – Who agrees to that?

She said (at the time) she was over him, so this guy and I started dating, mostly just for fun. I didn't think it was going to go anywhere, since he was such a bad boy. But it got heated and intense quickly. Then our friend decided she didn't want to bless us anymore. She wanted him back, leaving us in some sort of limbo and not sure what to do. We laid low for a bit, but one night we got caught making out at a club. We were all over the tabloids at that point—a big spread with multiple photos and several pages—and even though she'd revoked the blessing, it was a bit too late. We were into it pretty deeply with each other.

Lindsay – I must say, you guys did look pretty hot in those photos. And wow. Anyone around you could not deny the sex oozing from both of you. There was major chemistry.

We did. It's true. And it was hot and heavy, plus I was eventually fully able to see the goodness in this guy. Or maybe I wanted to see it. We weren't sure how to proceed at that point. It had been three months into the relationship, but it was sweet and loving and had, in that time, moved at the speed of light.

> 66
> *Lindsay* – You did have that tiny nagging feeling that something wasn't exactly the way it should have been, though. Your gut was telling you something.

There was indeed a tiny part of me that thought it wasn't just right. Something. I thought that maybe, individually, we weren't mature enough to be in a relationship together. There weren't blatant reasons not to trust him, but I'd witnessed a certain pattern of behaviors that made me think, *Hmm, this isn't the behavior of a lifelong partner.* But we were having such a great time.

One weekend, while I was boarding a plane to meet my guy, my parents called to say hello. I thought they wanted to catch up. Instead, they had a big secret, which they were supposed to keep. They kept it for all of five seconds then told me that my guy had called them. "He's asked for your hand in marriage! He's going to propose," they told me on the phone.

I was flying to meet him in Vegas for New Year's Eve—I was coming from New York and he from LA. That meant, likely, he called them to ask, thinking I was on a plane already and not with them, and that I was going to be proposed to in Vegas. *Oh no.* In my gut and mind all that I kept hearing was: *Abort! Abort! Don't board the plane!* But I did have strong feelings for him, and if I did a no-show, it would have been over.

> 66
> *Lindsay* – I have to admit, I was a bit worried because this guy didn't like me so much. I think he felt our friendship got in the way of their relationship. But I was

excited to know I was going to be helping plan a wedding. I
remember thinking: I hope he starts to like me soon!

....

My parents and I are super close. They had a lot of questions and wanted me to take my time. Their concern was that I was nowhere near the marriage phase. The problem was, while they may have been right, I also wasn't ready to break up with him either. So there I was boarding a plane, with my head spinning, hearing news from my parents I wasn't supposed to know. Thoughts were going crazy in my brain:

If I say no, is that the end of the relationship?

If I say yes, will it work?

Knowing this guy, where else can this go, other than marriage? It's all in or all out.

What am I going to do?

What am I supposed to do?

It was the most stressful and yet somehow exciting plane ride I've ever taken. I freaked out for the entire five-hour flight. But in that time, I came up with a solution. If indeed he did propose, I was going to say yes but suggest that we spend a couple of years being engaged, so we could really get to know each other. I realized I did truly love him. That I knew. And I wasn't ready to say good-bye. I thought my solution was great. We wouldn't set a date. It wasn't a 100 percent YES! But it was a very, very solid maybe. Then, of course, even though I'd settled on my solution, somewhere over the middle of the country, I started thinking of not only the good qualities he had but also the not-so-good ones, the ones I wasn't sure I could live with. My mind was going as fast as the plane.

I was big on loyalty—always have been, maybe to a fault. With this relationship, I wasn't sure about his loyalty. And I'm not talking about cheating. I mean loyalty as having a partner in everything called life. Sometimes, he felt competitive with me. That was weird. A mature relationship shouldn't be that. A little bit is healthy, sure, but it shouldn't be the essence of a relationship. Sometimes, with us, I felt like it was. Could I trust him in business? I wasn't sure about that either. I also understood he had a huge family and they depended on him heavily, but I also felt he was torn between his loyalty to them and to me. And marrying this guy meant marrying his forty-person-deep clan. My family is my mom, my dad, and my dog. We're quiet and private. His was different. His was all-involved. Suddenly, I was feeling overwhelmed. And he hadn't even proposed yet!

Finally, the plane landed—the longest plane ride in history. One drink usually gets me all happy and excited, so I didn't have one. I wanted a clear head. He had sent a limo to the airport to greet me. I got to the hotel and two men met me and walked me up to a suite—he'd booked the Wynn Hotel. *Damn, he went all out.*

I finally walked into this gorgeous suite. He greeted me and walked me along rose petals that led from one room to the next. I followed them to the bedroom and there was a huge heart made out of rose petals on the bed. There was champagne and a bubble bath with rose petals. It was beautiful.

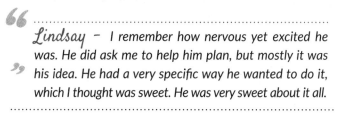

Lindsay – I remember how nervous yet excited he was. He did ask me to help him plan, but mostly it was his idea. He had a very specific way he wanted to do it, which I thought was sweet. He was very sweet about it all.

The entire plan was beautiful and thoughtful. I realized, *we're getting straight to the point here. I guess my parents were right?* He clearly wasn't waiting until dinner or anything like that.

Then, it got really cute. Despite all of the planning and romance that went into it, something sweet and funny happened. We sat on the edge of the bed. He gave me a Louis Vuitton bag—limited edition. It was a beautiful gift and I thanked him for it.

"Open it," he said.

I was dying inside. *Oh my God, Oh my God, Oh my God. This is it. This is it. This is happening!* I took out a little envelope that contained the bag number for authenticity.

"No, not the envelope. The box," he said.

Shoot. Here we go. I took out a little box from inside the bag. I opened the box and inside was the most beautiful ring. It was three or so carats. A solid diamond rock in the center with little baguettes all around. I later learned he designed it himself. I looked up at him, smiling.

He was just sitting there smiling. He was looking at me, but not saying anything.

"Wow, this is a gorgeous ring," I said. And looked back at him.

Nothing. He smiled. He looked nervous. If he wasn't going to propose, it was a cruel trick, because, to me, it looked like an engagement ring. There was no mistaking that. Still, he said nothing.

"It's so beautiful," I said again.

Nothing.

It was getting slightly more awkward by the second. "So," I said. "Does this . . . mean anything?"

Another pause. Then finally he said, "Yes."

It was awkward enough that I seriously contemplated thanking him for the present and then switching subjects.

He paused for one more second, then finally asked, "Will you make me the happiest man on earth? *Could* you marry me?" He had frozen up when I first opened the ring and then he even messed up the question!

I was so excited but so grateful I'd had the plane time to come up with an answer. I immediately did my whole shebang: I told him we should take our time and not rush, but that I did want to spend my life with him, that we didn't need to lock into a day, but that we could live together and do it all when we were ready and blah, blah, blah. Surprisingly, he took it really well. We laughed forever about how he was unable to actually ask the question. It was cute.

— The Over-Analyzation —

Karina

The engagement lasted six months, and then we broke up. After he proposed, it seemed like he heard me, but then he was ready and raring to go, not so eager to wait and get to know one another. Looking back, he was probably upset by my answer and I don't blame him. If reversed, if I were in his shoes, I wouldn't have taken that response so well. I wore the ring, but he probably knew my heart wasn't 100 percent in it. Plus, as time went by, it was clear we weren't giving and taking, like a normal couple. We were pushing and pulling. That wasn't grounds or a base for a healthy marriage. We started learning a lot about each other in the months that followed, and a lot of it was stuff that neither of us was ever going to learn to deal with. That's why relationships need time. You need a year to figure each other out.

Lindsay

I would agree. It was so cute that he forgot his words. He was truly in love. It just showed that he was human and emotional about Karina. I wanted Karina to be happy, but these two were competitive with each other and that didn't seem like the recipe for a successful marriage. At the same time, yes, he must have felt a little hurt by her answer. I wouldn't want that answer if I expressed my love like that. But honesty is the best policy, and I want someone to be straight with me more than anything. I think he appreciated that at the end of the day. I also think they dated ahead of their time. These two have always had an intense connection. To this day, even after a lot of tears and a very difficult breakup, they have a deep bond that is undeniable. Had all of it happened today, I believe they would have made it to "I do." This is the kind of passion, drama, love, and chemistry that seems to only happen in the movies.

Guy's Corner

Jacoby

I have bad knees from football. So I wouldn't have been able to get down on one knee. As for missing the question: It's possible. Karina might have made him nervous. She's beautiful. Me: I'd get the job done, though.

Ricardo

I think it's cute. I hope the ring was big.

Lindsay and Karina

This story is from our fabulously talented, funny, and amazing friend Lisa Ann Walter. She's an experienced actress, writer, comedian, and now, online dater. One of the things that both of us have learned from Lisa Ann is the importance of confidence. Own what you have and who you are. Be who you are because why would you want to end up with a guy who likes you for being someone you're not? She approaches everything with a spicy humor, and there's never a dull moment when we're all together.

Can't-Stop-Talking Guy

Lisa Ann Walter, Actress, Writer, Comedian, LA

Four kids, multiple frog kisses, and lots of peer pressure later, I decided that, for the first time in my life, I would make the foray into online dating. One of my best friends—an absolutely stunning actress who starred in *Strong Medicine*, among other shows—was doing it and she suggested I try it. But she's so gorgeous she's fishing with a different kind of bait than I am. She's grade A. It's like Karina dating. I'm like, "How did you guys have a bad date, unless the guy is a big liar or you, ya know, made idiotic choices?" It just didn't seem possible. In this case, my friend went on Match.com, and I thought it was hilarious that she literally put her picture up for twenty-four hours and had some kind of crazy response in the range of five thousand guys. She went through half of the pages on Match. com, picked out two guys, and went on a lunch date with one—no chemistry. The second one she married.

"

Lindsay – I can relate to the mass of e-mails. There's never enough time to get through all of them. I haven't been on Match in years and I'm still getting e-mails.

"

Even though I cancelled my subscription years ago, they never deleted it. Some day when I'm married, my husband is going to have to flex his muscle and demand that it be removed. I've tried and they keep giving me the runaround. So I keep getting e-mails that I can't respond to. I wish date number two was it for me.

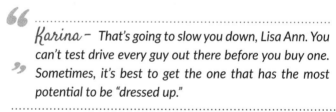

Karina – *That doesn't happen to anybody. C'mon. That's just great luck. This should be a commercial. Come on Match.com. This is a golden story. The story that leads us to believe, hope, and try . . . forever!*

My first thought when she told me that she found her guy was, *How in the world could she not go through all the options first?* Women are shoppers. We're berry pickers. It's like shopping for shoes at the mall—I have to see all of them before I decide I found the right ones.

Karina – *That's going to slow you down, Lisa Ann. You can't test drive every guy out there before you buy one. Sometimes, it's best to get the one that has the most potential to be "dressed up."*

Well, my hot friend found her guy and that was it. She liked the chemistry, they made out in the car, and she decided: "I'm going to marry this one." And she did. I performed the ceremony for them! That convinced me that I should try online dating.

So I did. My first mistake was letting my friend put up my profile because she aged me down about 15 percent. She insisted, "No, no, no, no, you have no idea. You go on Match and guys lie about two things," she said. "Their income and their hair. They're all bald. Every guy you see with a hat in his picture is bald." And she said, "Women lie about their age. It's perfectly okay."

Lindsay – Men lie about their height, too.

Yup. Two inches. So I thought: You know what? I think it's rude to ask a woman her age on a first date anyway. It wouldn't happen in real life! You wouldn't go out with someone and say, "So I thought we might see a movie. . . . By the way, how old are you?" Just as it would be rude to ask the gentleman certain statistics. "Hi, I'm Lisa, you have a nice profile. How big is your dick?" Really? You wouldn't say, "How much do you make in a year? Net. How much do you make, net?" You just wouldn't do it. Plus, in my profession, age is the enemy. So, suffice it to say, she aged my profile down a little bit. It is, after all, LA. LA—where prom queens go to die. So that does a couple of things. It spoils the shit out of the men because their Denny's waitress was a prom queen. Everybody was a prom queen. Their dental hygienist was Miss Junior Minneapolis. Everybody was told that they were the cutest girl in their hometown, so they came out to Hollywood to be an actress, and that's why the men are so spoiled in this town. It's unbelievable—frickin' Quasimodo guys think they have a shot at you. And they're seventy. And they're broke. And you see it everywhere. The guy from Jiffy Lube thinks that he's going to bang Carmen Electra. That's what he thinks he deserves. The guys that are asking you out are crazy-looking and sort of nutty. There's an extra layer of work for us out here because we have to weed through what they're writing on these profiles to see where the crazy is. Sometimes I can figure it out. Sometimes I can avoid it. And sometimes I can't.

When I first got started with online dating, I also observed that these guys posted stupid photos of themselves. Lots of them put pictures of their Harleys up there. I'm certain these were photos of all the stuff their wives didn't let them do when they were married. They're trying to get women by posting pics that basically read: "I'm having a midlife crisis. Look, here's all my big boy stuff!" We don't care about your stupid toys! If this was "Match-up-with-dudes-to-go-riding-dot-com," then it'd be fine. But it's not. Hey, I don't post pictures of my favorite handbags up there. Note to online daters: I don't give a shit about your motorcycle.

Once I got into the actual dating, I would meet a guy who had an okay picture without a Harley in it, and I found I was talking myself into some of them. Part of my decision was based on whether or not I could picture myself sweating under the guy. I learned quickly that if I was sitting across from someone and I found that I was talking myself into it, then I couldn't do it. It's not like you're meeting in a club and the energy and the chemistry is pumping, so you're totally into the guy—then you find you're talking yourself into other stuff. Like when he says his "band is going to take off really soon." Cut to this sexy, unemployed guy who's moved him and his guitar into your house. But if the basic attraction isn't even there. . . . If you're thinking, *Maybe I could bring myself to kiss this guy even though he has yellow teeth,* then it's time to acknowledge, immediately, that you can't. That's what I found as I sifted through the dates. I wasn't up for that compromise.

I came across one guy who appeared okay. A few red flags—like he said he worked in "medicine." Here's the deal with Match: The field of "medicine" can mean he's an actual doctor—like a neurosurgeon—or it can mean he's a trainer at Gold's Gym. It can mean anything. Also, they all say they make over $150,000 a year. To be clear, I am not looking for a man to take care of me, but I am also not prepared to go back down the road that I've been on in every other relationship where I was the one making the money and then I wound up taking care of everyone. I'm too cute for that. It's ridiculous.

When I began online dating, I just wanted to find a guy with his shit together. He didn't have to be a multimillionaire. They always turn out to be a pain in the ass anyway. Trust me: When you marry money, you earn every penny. I just wanted a normal guy with a career that he was passionate about, who had a shekel to rub together. If there's too much disparity in income, then the guy is threatened by you.

❝
Lindsay – Equal at the very least. I don't want to support a guy. Been there, done that, and it's stressful.
❞

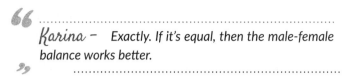

Karina – *Exactly. If it's equal, then the male-female balance works better.*

This guy and I agreed to meet for a lunch date. It was perfect because I knew I could squeeze it in before I had to volunteer for the snack bar at my twins' football game. I met him at the door of P.F. Chang's (his choice). A few observations:

His hair was totally unkempt. It was like he styled it with a NutriBullet.

His teeth were a disaster. Yellow. All sorts of wrong was happening in that mouth. If you're making over $150,000 a year get that stuff sorted out.

His shirt was unbuttoned halfway down his chest, so there was sloppy gray chest hair poking out. I started hearing disco music in my head and was thinking, *where are the gold chains?*

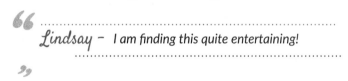

Lindsay – *I am finding this quite entertaining!*

I wanted to leave, but I couldn't do that. You can't look someone in the face and say, "Eww." I would never be that rude. But I wanted to, believe me! Still, we sat down and he just launched into his big brag. He was a psychiatrist. "I can prescribe meds," he said proudly.

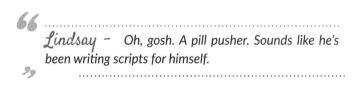

Lindsay – *Oh, gosh. A pill pusher. Sounds like he's been writing scripts for himself.*

He was explaining his job to me as if I was a semi-special needs case. And then he was telling me that his big thing—the one thing—the thing that made him a catch was that he could get me Adderall under the table. Seriously.

175

He kept going on about it. I mean, we're in the Valley surrounded by women with too much Botox and all happy to abuse their own kids' stash of Adderall, so I'm sure he thought I'd be jumping at it like a dog on peanut butter. He went on and on for ten minutes before I finally pointed out that **a)** I could get it anywhere, but abusing a drug for off-label purposes was, um, ethically wrong, and **b)** I was sober seven years so that wasn't a big selling point for me. Still, he kept going and going. And he twitched every thirty seconds or so. His shoulder had a twitch. I thought perhaps he had Tourette. Since he talked and talked and talked, I started having a conversation in my head: *I think people with Tourette's twitch. Maybe he has it. Wonder if he'll start sprouting curse words.* I was also thinking: *I'm usually the one doing the talking. I'm not shy and I have no issue jumping in on any conversation. But, wow, I can't get a word in edgewise with a crowbar.* It was never going to happen.

Forty minutes went by, and every time I tried to add to the conversation, he actually interrupted and said, "Let me finish." He had nonstop verbal diarrhea. Of course, he failed at his job to make sure I had food or a drink—a biological imperative for a guy on a date at mealtime. Feed your mate. So I let him keep rambling, while I flagged down the waiter and ordered. (Sidebar: I went on another Match.com date, and when I got there, the guy had already ordered himself two drinks and started eating without me. He didn't even ask if I wanted a soda.)

So Adderall guy didn't bother asking, "Are you hungry?" I hadn't had breakfast; I'd dropped the kids off at school and done my errands. I was expecting to eat. The nice part was that I was able to finish my entire meal in peace, just eating, without having to break to add to what became this ridiculous one-sided monologue. I literally ate my entire meal without worrying I'd spit food out on my date. He didn't ask me a single question about me or my life or my kids. Nothing. In my head, while I stared and listened to his ramble, I wondered if he had self-medicated or if he was on cocaine and couldn't stop talking because a lot of psychiatrists use blow—as they aspire to be Sigmund Freud.

This guy was either coked out of his mind or he was just the worst person at deciphering social cues that I've ever met in my life. Literally, I could not speak. It was the worst Match.com date ever.

And then it just got worse. Just when I thought it was over and I said, "I have to go pick up my kids," he launched into something new that I hadn't expected. It became apparent he'd researched me and knew who I was pre date.

He started barraging me with: "Let me ask you a question. Do you know this guy? Do you know this guy?" And then it took him forever to find the picture as he sat there, and I was trying to talk to say "No" and "I really gotta go," and he kept saying, "Wait, wait. Let me finish." He finally showed me a picture and I said, "No, I'm sorry, I don't know him." More questions: "You don't know him? You don't know him? You don't know this person?" Me: "No. I don't." At this point, I started to get very nervous, wondering if this guy was with the FBI or something, and I'd been set up. "I have never met this person," I insisted.

"It's my brother," he said. "You dated him ten years ago."

Huh?

"I'm sorry, I've never met him."

"You must know him. You don't know him?" he asked again. "You were introduced during the blah blah blah. By blah blah blah."

Shoot me.

Then he decided that maybe I didn't date him, maybe I just met him. Through work. "He's in the industry." That's when I knew that he knew I was an actress. Not that he'd taken the time to ask exactly and have a conversation about my actual work like a normal person.

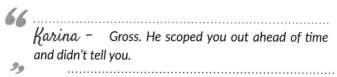

Karina – Gross. He scoped you out ahead of time and didn't tell you.

It was clear that his brother had seen my picture already. I continued to apologize and pretend that I was the jerk for not recognizing him, insisting it was because I met so many people. I wanted to say, "I'm an actress. If he works in the industry on a project that I'm on, it would be your brother's job to know who I am. How am I supposed to remember everybody I meet?" But I didn't. I didn't want to look like an asshole. It was better at this point that only he looked like an asshole.

The best part of all of this was that after a disastrous and painful lunch and monologue (keep in mind this is maybe my fifth Match date), he walked me to my car and said, "I think we could have a lot of fun together—when do you want to go out again?" I thought, *what do you need me for? You can have this conversation all by yourself and save the twelve bucks for the Chinese Chicken Salad.*

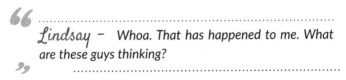

Lindsay – Whoa. That has happened to me. What are these guys thinking?

This happened a lot. It was a trend. Karina—you'll get a kick out of this. There was one guy I dated before Adderall guy. He told me he was a body builder. Nice enough. He was a good dancer. We were dancing and he was taking the lead. He was a strong lead, too. He did country. The Texas Two-Step, which I'd never done, but it's an easy-as-hell dance. There was some line dancing happening, and I picked it up quickly. Out of nowhere, he started manhandling me on the dance floor. It was so aggressive and crazy I finally said to him, "I'm sorry to be rude, but do you juice? Do you do steroids?" His answer: "You know, I'm not going to lie to you. I do." He was throwing me around the dance floor like cheap lawn furniture! I felt like I was physically being attacked.

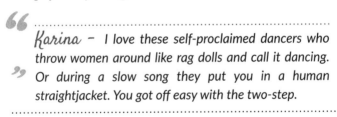

Karina – I love these self-proclaimed dancers who throw women around like rag dolls and call it dancing. Or during a slow song they put you in a human straightjacket. You got off easy with the two-step.

At the end of that date he said, "I'm taking my profile down. I think you and I are going be exclusive. We'd have a great life together." By the way, he also did not have a home. He was sleeping at his gym. So I guess our great life would be taking place at my house!

Lindsay and Karina

Kira is one of our favorite people. She is also one of the wittiest people on earth. The three of us have had many laughs over tons of guys and dates gone wrong. She's been there through thick and thin and is proof now, as a happily married woman to the most incredible hubby and father, that when you stick to your guns, have faith, and be open to finding "the one" even in the most unexpected of places, true love still exists.

More-Time-in-the-Mirror-Than-Me Guy

Kira, Branding Manager, LA

I met this guy from out of state while he was in LA for an awards show party. He was a handsome, sweet, successful country singer, and after a week of spending time together, I thought I felt a spark between us. We hadn't spent any time alone, but we had fun in a group setting that week—laughing and hanging out casually. He returned home at the end of the week. We talked a bit and texted long distance, until I finally decided to get on a plane and visit him a few months after we'd originally met.

I booked my ticket to Nashville, knowing everything would be great because, well, why wouldn't it be?

66

Lindsay – This is going to be good. Giddy up! Yee-haw!

99

66

Karina – Uh-oh. Getting on a plane to go see him this early in the relationship is optimistic and ambitious.

99

We'd had good conversations and really connected every time we'd spoken on the phone. How wrong could I have been? From the moment that he picked me up at the airport, he was a totally different person. It was like Dr. Jekyll and Mr. Hyde—as if I had arrived and was speaking with someone completely different than I'd met. He wasn't fun and chatty. He was shy and awkward. That's not a bad thing, but it wasn't the guy I'd gotten to know in Los Angeles.

When we arrived at his house, like the switch of a light, he was back to being the guy I'd met originally—talking and lively. But there was something different. He only spoke about himself. Obsessively. He was suddenly self-absorbed to an extent I'd never before quite experienced. He couldn't stop name-dropping, talking about what a huge musician he was (he was D list at best). Everything in his room was about him: pictures of him on stage, performing, backstage. It was almost a shrine of him—right there in the bedroom. He didn't show me the pictures like they were historical or interesting. Instead, he spoke about them to me as if he were introducing me to the world of celebrity, unaware I worked in the business and was unfazed by any of it. He went into his closet and pulled out one outfit after another to tell me what he wore when. It was the craziest thing I'd ever experienced. I just nodded. There was nothing to say except, of course, "Get over yourself." None of it impressed me. Nothing he had to say was remotely interesting, and it was shocking to think that he couldn't stop himself for one second to talk about anything else.

There was a girl at his place visiting or staying with him. A friend of the family or something. She was young and obsessed with the guy. Obsessed. She clung to us, batting her eyelashes at him, feeding his ego. It was so strange that he was okay having her there while I was there, but then again, she was so into him, telling him how great he was all the time, he was probably happy to have her around.

He let me get settled before we left for dinner. But it wasn't to give me the time. I realized after I was ready in ten minutes that he needed a full hour. I sat there waiting for him in the living room. When we finally headed out to a local place, he created this persona: walking like everyone was looking at him because he was so famous. But no one really noticed him. He kept saying, "Oh, everyone's staring at me." But they simply weren't. Maybe they were looking at my amazing dress, but not at him. He wasn't recognizable enough.

Even in his own town. He had toured, that I knew, but he certainly wasn't a household name. Maybe a small crowd in Nashville might know who he was, but no one at the restaurant did.

During the entire dinner he just talked about himself. The discussion ranged from his big dreams and aspirations down to what he ate for breakfast. It wasn't just startling at that point, it was downright offensive. I couldn't take it anymore.

I couldn't get out of that restaurant fast enough. When we finally left and we were in the car, I asked if we could stop at the wine store to get something to drink at home. I needed one badly. "Oh, sorry. It's Sunday. In Tennessee, there's no liquor on Sunday. I've got some booze at home, though," he said.

Well, that turned out to be an overstatement. There were bottles, sure, but every single one—and I'm not exaggerating here—every single bottle on his bar cart had less than half an inch of liquid in it. When I did take a little pour of one, it was watered down. He'd poured water in them to stretch them out. I figured he was keeping the fancy bottles on the counter so he looked fancy, but clearly there was a money issue or something, because there was no booze in that house. I thought I was going to die. He did pay for dinner, but he couldn't afford to have enough booze to help me forget about my misery.

Another thing he couldn't afford: toilet paper. He had none in the house. Every time I went into the bathroom, he tore up pieces of paper towel for me. It was so insanely gross.

I stayed in the same room with him, and while he wanted to have sex, I did not. So we didn't. It was weird and awkward, to say the least. I was relieved when he told me he had to leave to do a little work that morning. I was grateful to have some time to myself. But that changed quickly. That irritating girl came into his room and sat on his bed. While I was in it.

At this point, all I wanted to say to her was to leave me alone. I didn't. She peppered me with questions:

Her: "What are you doing today?"
Me: "I don't know. I don't have a car, and I have no clue where I am."
Her: "Do you like him?"
Me: "I don't know."

At this point, I was starting to think that I was being punked. I actually started looking around for hidden cameras in the room, thinking this absolutely had to be some sort of test. That he thought it was important to send a twenty-year-old-who-should-be-an-adult-and-know-better in to talk to me while I was in my underwear and a tank top in bed. It was horrifying. The inquisition went on for a solid hour.

When she finally left, I realized I absolutely had to make a run for it and get out of there. I knew I couldn't stay for one more second. I packed up my suitcase and I headed into the bathroom to get ready. I opened one drawer to find toothpaste, and I realized the entire cabinet was full of bronzer and primping products. Loads of them. At first I wondered if it was all there to serve all the girls he had coming in (a notion I was completely fine and comfortable with), but then as I snooped a little, I realized it was all for him. There was man mascara, man makeup—man everything. It made sense. He was as vain as they came and his vanity items took up the entire bathroom. It wasn't on his bus or backstage, it was at his home. This was his lifestyle—a bathroom full of stuff usually reserved for a sixteen-year-old girl.

It was all too much to handle. I called the airline. I had one night left to stay, but I figured out when the flights were leaving that day. I decided I would head to the airport and get on an earlier flight. I called myself a car to pick me up from his place and take me to the airport. A few minutes the driver called to say he'd arrived at the gate. The guy lived in a gated community. To get in, you needed to phone his cell. To get out, I assumed it would just open with motion. The walk to the gate was too far—maybe half a mile. A twenty-minute walk. His house was one of the farthest away. When I finally reached the gate, I could see my car, but I couldn't get myself out. There was no security guard, nothing. I contemplated climbing under or over the fence, but that was not going to happen. It was too high and too low at the same time.

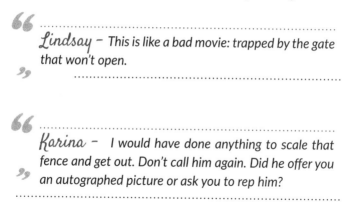

Lindsay – This is like a bad movie: trapped by the gate that won't open.

Karina – I would have done anything to scale that fence and get out. Don't call him again. Did he offer you an autographed picture or ask you to rep him?

As I stood there, jumping around, trying to find a motion detector, my phone rang. It was him. He was on his way back. I hadn't told him I was leaving because I didn't want to deal with the discussion and feel uncomfortable. I just wanted to disappear quietly. So when he called, I reacted the same way. I just said, "Okay, I'll see you soon." And I ran the half-mile back to his house, dragging my suitcase behind me, abandoning my cab and my dignity.

As quickly as I could, out of breath and disheveled, I re-unpacked so it didn't look like I'd packed up anything. Just as I finished, he walked in the door. From there, I endured another eighteen hours of listening to him talk about his dead-end, oh-so-dull, mediocre career. I listened once again to his tales of being on stage performing, his phenomenal career, how he was the biggest thing in the world, and so on. The entire time I was there, he did not ask me one single question about myself. If we even weaved remotely off course about any other topic, he promptly returned to his favorite subject: himself.

I woke up early the next morning and told him it was time to leave, that I had gotten a call and had to head back a little early. Some lie, something I can't even remember. The earliest flight I could switch to was at noon, but I left his house at 7:30 a.m. It was more interesting to go and spend four hours at the Nashville airport than to listen to one more word out of this guy's mouth. And I accepted the only remaining seat: a middle one.

> *Karina* – *You know it is bad when you take a middle seat. Not all escapes are perfect. You should have hidden behind a tree and run out when the gate opened for his car. Have you suggested he date himself? It would be the perfect match.*

After that fiasco of a weekend, he continued to call. I said it wasn't going to work out, but still, he asked if we could at least be friends. I told him no. I had enough friends.

From Karina's Mom

We need to teach our daughters to know the difference between:

A man who flatters her and a man who compliments her.

A man who spends money on her and a man who invests in her.

A man who views her as property and a man who views her properly.

A man who lusts after her and a man who loves her.

A man who believes he's a gift to women, and a man who believes she's a gift to him.

And then we need to teach our sons to be that kind of man.

Chapter 10:
No Worries, I'm All Good Here

I-Haven't-Eaten-in-Weeks Guy

Lindsay

In online dating, women are more often pursued than men. After a guy messaged me, I scanned his profile quickly to check qualities—I was less about the photo, more about common ground. There was one guy who contacted me who seemed okay. He wasn't a stunner, but we had a lot in common and he had piercing blue eyes. I was at the stage where I was trying to put myself out there, as my mom said to do, so I responded. It was on eHarmony so we did some back and forth, which can take some time. When we got to the e-mailing stage, I was in New York. Karina was on Broadway and we were there for the summer. We seemed to be hitting it off. He said, "When you get back, I'd love to take you out."

I agreed. Back in LA, we settled on a place in Century City. It was during the week, so we agreed to meet in the bar around five o'clock. Now, I never get there early. Ever. But I was. I'm usually just a few minutes late. I sat down and scanned the crowd, but I didn't see him anywhere. After a few minutes, I texted him. It turned out he was there, too. He told me he was wearing flannel. Since he was the only guy there wearing flannel, we connected finally. He was easy to spot then. The reason I didn't see him immediately when I got there was that he looked nothing like his photo. Those blue eyes had clearly been color enhanced, and unlike his photo, he was tired (like he hadn't slept in days), scraggly, his hair was long and messy, and he hadn't shaved.

We sat in a booth. He'd already had a beer so he had the tab transferred to our table.

"Are you hungry?" he asked.

"Not really. It's early. Should we split an appetizer and get some drinks?" I asked.

"Sure. What do you like?"

"I don't eat beef and I can't eat wheat," I said.

The waitress came by. He ordered five appetizers including nachos with beef, Kobe beef sliders, mahimahi tacos, edamame hummus with pita chips, and something else I can't remember.

The waitress left and I asked, "Can we get some veggies, maybe? So I can dip into the hummus?" He said yes, but we never did.

I knew within minutes that this date was going nowhere. We were struggling. There was nothing to talk about except surfing. It was the only common interest we had and I'm not even interested in it. But it was the only topic I could add a little bit to. Meanwhile, this guy was going to town on the food, like he had not eaten in weeks. He was circling the selection, taking one bite from each plate. He even grabbed up three of the six tomatoes on the hummus plate, the only thing there I could eat.

I thought it was clear to us both we were just filling time. But as I was plotting how I was going to escape, he actually ordered a second drink. I was shocked. He couldn't have been enjoying the date any more than I was. We had nothing to say. I assumed he just wanted to prolong it so he could keep eating.

"I have to check my phone, I'm sorry. My son is with a sitter," I said.

I left the table and made a fake phone call.

"I'm so sorry," I said upon return. "We have to get the bill. I've got to be home by six o'clock."

The bill arrived. And it just sat there. This guy had ordered enough food to feed a small family, and he wasn't making a move to pay for it at all.

I finally picked up the bill. He said, "Do you want to split it?"

"No, that's fine. I got it."

"Thanks," he said.

"No worries," I said. "No worries at all."

" ....

Karina – *That's our code for "fuck off." If we say "no worries," it means "fuck you, and you should be worrying."*

" ....

I got out of there as quickly as I could.

" ....

Karina – *And he got a free meal that should have filled him up for the week. Maybe online dating is just to support his eating habits.*

....

— The Over-Analyzati**on** —

Lindsay ....

Here's the thing: When you're a parent, time takes on a new value. Your child is the person you want to spend time with and it's hard to convince yourself to go on a ton of dates. Then when you end up on one that's going nowhere, you no longer make those same excuses. You no longer feel like just being entertained. In this case, I didn't want to waste one more second with said guy because I knew I was completely over it. Once I knew that, I was out.

Karina ....

A dear friend of mine, my makeup artist on the show, has had a very colorful dating life. She's been married five times and engaged nine times. And naturally, when I'm in her chair I love getting her perspective on things. Once, she told me to sit down by myself in a quiet room and write down a thorough description of what I would consider to be my ideal man. She said to be very specific and then read it to God and release it to the universe. Well, needless to say, I followed her instructions. And soon after I met (*who-I-thought-then-was*) a great guy. Soon after I realized that the quality in him I really didn't like was one of the few qualities I didn't write down in my letter to God. So I rewrote my letter and did the entire process again. Soon after I met another (*who-I-thought-then-was-a*) great man. And guess what? He revealed a trait that I just couldn't live with. Again, something I hadn't covered in my letter. I had to rewrite it again. You need to cover yourself on all fronts and the "letter" has to be so descriptive and detailed that you even include avoiding those who can't sustain their own eating habits. This guy who had dinner at Lindsay's expense definitely is a poster child for bottom feeders. Bright future ahead.

Guy's Corner

Ricardo

She shouldn't have paid. She should have sat there and stared, or gotten up to go to the bathroom to powder her nose. Anything. This guy was just rude. He didn't order anything she'd eat and then just waited for his free meal? Terrible.

Lindsay

Lesley called me the day after this date, and I can't say I was shocked. Online dating definitely ups your numbers in terms of dates, but it also adds a whole new component to dating. You're taking people at their word on everything. Height, age, education level, income, likes, and dislikes, and even many of the photos aren't accurate or they're from twenty years earlier. I never get it. Do men and women who lie online really think that's going to up their chances of finding love? And instead of doing it for free the old-fashioned way, with online dating, you're paying to lie to people? I find the whole thing rather odd. And then with guys who not only lie, but then have obvious mental issues, like this guy—that's when you start to really wonder: *Am I really upping my chances? Or am I just wasting valuable time going on a 21st-century* blind date? My rule of thumb for online dating is: Don't just interact minimally, make sure you have ample phone conversations first. Make sure he checks out and can hold an actual conversation about interesting and relevant things. Sure, I've absolutely ignored my own advice and that's why I have stories for several volumes of this book, but at the end of the day we need to date smarter and stop making rash decisions to accept dates prematurely.

Good Thing You Chose a Coffee Shop

Lesley, Fashion Marketer, LA

In my industry, most of the guys I work with are gay, so I have to go online to meet men. There's no other way to do it. One afternoon, I was looking online. I found one guy who looked cute—not the most gorgeous man I'd ever seen, but attractive enough. I wanted to find a nice guy—that was more important than super hot—so this guy seemed a good fit. Eventually, we communicated and planned our first meeting. He suggested several bars at which we could meet. All of them were hotel bars. That struck me as weird. My first thought was that he was hoping the drink would go well and I'd eventually go upstairs to a room with him. Every time I suggested something different, he got back to a hotel bar. In retrospect, we were meeting in Beverly Hills and a lot of bars there are in hotels. But still, it just seemed strange that he kept coming back to hotel bars.

After much back and forth, we finally settled on a location—The Coffee Bean & Tea Leaf. That was his suggestion and compromise to anything other than a hotel bar. I arrived before he did. When he did show up, he was about one foot shorter than his pictures and profile had implied. He looked dramatically different, too. I'd never been on an online date before where he looked so different from what was promised. Not only that, he was weirdly super shiny and sweaty. It was almost as though he'd rolled in something greasy. I tried not to focus on the sheen.

We went to the counter to place our orders. I asked for tea. He picked up a water bottle and handed it to the girl behind the counter.

I said to him, "No coffee or tea?"

He said, "No. I don't drink coffee or tea."

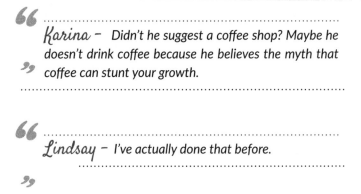

Karina – Didn't he suggest a coffee shop? Maybe he doesn't drink coffee because he believes the myth that coffee can stunt your growth.

Lindsay – I've actually done that before.

I was perplexed since he suggested The Coffee Bean, but whatever. We sat down and started talking. I mentioned something about having worked for a fashion company and that some remodeling was being done and they were moving to another state. It was sort of a throwaway conversation, just meant to fill in some blanks and make chitchat. Suddenly, out of nowhere, the date turned into a rapid-fire, intense interrogation. He peppered me with questions like:

Who did the construction?

How long did it take?

Do you know how much they spent?

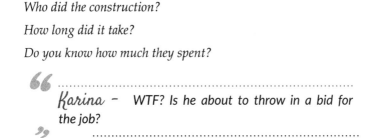

Karina – WTF? Is he about to throw in a bid for the job?

I was a little flustered. I couldn't give him the answers he wanted because I didn't really know. I wasn't that intricately involved in the process of the huge organization. It was incredibly strange. Still, he kept going and going and going. Nonstop. Trying to shift the conversation slightly, I said something about hiring some interns. Again, he fired off a round of questions:

Where did you get them?

What skill set do they have?

Do they have bookkeeping skills?

Do you have to train them a lot?

Lindsay – How weird. It's like you had black market top-secret interns or something. They're interns.

I tried to talk about anything else—the weather, the news—anything. But he kept steering the conversation back to the freaking construction and interns. It was all so strange, so I finally said, "I don't understand why you keep asking me about this. I'm trying to have a conversation and you keep going back to construction and interns. Is there a reason that you're obsessed with it?"

He came up with some answer about his business and construction and being curious about what he could get if he used interns, because he was trying to get as many as he could.

Lindsay - *How romantic!*

Maybe next time tell me that, so I don't think you have some weird construction fetish. Regardless, it was over before it began. I couldn't wait to get out of there. At the thirty-minute mark, I made my exit. We both said good-bye and walked to our cars. The funny thing was, he made a point to drive by me and honk and wave as I was still walking to mine. I feel certain he wanted me to see that he had a very nice car. I couldn't have cared less.

I was happy it was only a thirty-minute situation I was stuck in. It was my first coffee date, but it was over quickly. People put up a good front, and you can think they have their stuff together, but until you meet them in person, you'll never know if there is chemistry or if they're pretending to be something they're not. Or think they are.

When One Date at a Time Isn't Enough

Martina, TV Producer, LA

Like most young people do when they move to LA, I had a variety of small jobs to make ends meet while I struggled to land TV work. One gig was working as a bartender in a hotel. Some guy came into the bar one night. He was taking a driver's education course because he had gotten a ticket.

> **Karina** – We call that a good old-fashioned sign. And who says studying for a driver's education test while drinking is a bad idea?

Based on that fact alone, I should have known better. But he was stunningly gorgeous—just so good-looking—I ignored all the signs, and so when he asked me out, I agreed. A few nights later, we went to dinner. He said something about knowing he wanted to go out with me because if we had kids they'd be in the right gene pool.

I didn't say it out loud, but I thought, *what are you, a Nazi? You chose me for my baby-making abilities before even knowing me? And you bring this up on the first date?*

To be clear, he wasn't being funny. He was clear that he looked at me mainly for my characteristics for our future.

"I wanted to be sure that if I were to have a child, my child would be pretty," he said.

> **Lindsay** – Lindsay Is that a wannabe compliment? Run!

Not remotely surprisingly, he was super vain, and at the end of the date, we went back to the bar where I worked and sat there in the lounge.

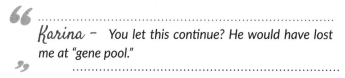

Karina – *You let this continue? He would have lost me at "gene pool."*

He went up to the bar to get us some drinks. It was very crowded, but still it seemed like he had spent a little bit too much time up there. It was quite a while before he returned. When he finally got back, we had our drinks, and the date ended. He was matter-of-fact about it all, like, "Okay, let's do this." No romance or anything, and I wasn't involved in the decision he'd made that we'd date.

The next day I went to work. My friend who had been bartending the night before said, "That guy you went out with last night. What's the story with him?"

"What do you mean?" I asked. "Why do you ask?"

"Well, is it serious?" she asked.

I was confused. I explained it was our first date, and a weird one at that.

"Well," she said, "when he came up to get the drinks he asked for my phone number and wanted to set up a date for later that night. I didn't go because I thought I'd check with you first."

He was attempting to make another date while he was on a date with me.

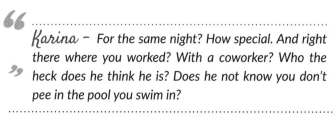

Karina – *For the same night? How special. And right there where you worked? With a coworker? Who the heck does he think he is? Does he not know you don't pee in the pool you swim in?*

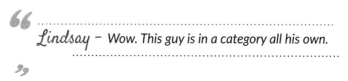

Lindsay – Wow. This guy is in a category all his own.

It was shocking, considering he knew where I worked, but I assumed that since he saw my horrific and disgusted look when he told me about our gene pool connection, he probably just wanted to hedge his bets for the night to be safe.

Lessons Learned from Lindsay's Mom

Look for the guy who is nice to the elderly and children (not just because it's convenient).

. . . .

Look for the guy who is compassionate.

. . . .

Watch out for the manipulators. They trick you. They'll tell you what you want to hear.

. . . .

Always look for honesty. If he's not honest in everything, he's not honest in anything.

. . . .

Seek integrity.

. . . .

If they don't have any faith, they're not big thinkers. Something has to be bigger than them. If not then nothing will ever be bigger in their mind than themselves.

. . . .

Chapter 11:
Best Kiss Ever

Lindsay and Karina

It is such a gift to have such an amazing group of girlfriends who we can laugh with and cry with, who we can gossip with, and who we can dream with. Most important, it's so nice to have friends in our lives that we can be happy for when things go right. That's why we decided to end on a super positive note by sharing some of our most memorable kisses ever. Lea's story reminded us that we do have to kiss a lot of frogs, but there are also Prince Charmings out there. And when we finally meet the man of our dreams, all of the frogs will have been worth it. Otherwise, how can we identify a true love's kiss if we haven't kissed the duds? Most of us don't have Lindsay's dad's luck (notice: didn't say Mom, too) of only ever kissing one person and knowing he or she is the one. So here's to all of our perpetual searches for love and happiness, and to lots of incredible lip-locking!

It's All about the Kiss

Lea Thompson, Actress, LA

In my lifetime, I have had three amazing *first* kisses. My first was my actual first kiss. Ever. I was twelve years old. We were at the Guthrie Theater doing a play called *Love's Labour's Lost*—four girls and two guys were in one of the dressing rooms, of all things, playing spin the bottle. At the time, I had a really big crush on my girlfriend's boyfriend. He was one of the two boys. The boys had the better odds, obviously. It was my turn to spin. I gave the bottle a whirl and my heart almost skipped a beat when it landed on him— my big crush. Nervously, I kissed him and then the entire world just spun around me. It was so amazing. The most amazing kiss ever. So much so that I couldn't eat for an entire day afterward.

"

Lindsay – That's the best feeling ever.

"

We stayed together for two years after that, dating as it were at age twelve—and to this day, he's still my friend. His girlfriend, my friend, well, she wasn't so happy.

Years later when I was seventeen, I was doing a play called *The Little Mermaid*. It was the story of the little mermaid and the prince—neither realizing they loved one another. It was super tragic. I did the play for five months with the same guy as my leading man. After his last night in the show, after months of pent-up lust, he walked into my dressing room, grabbed me, and kissed me for three minutes. It was so crazy and intense; I've remembered it forever.

I had one more kiss that was as crazy and intense, and that was with my husband. We were both working on a movie together, and at the time, I was engaged to someone else. My husband had a crush on me, and we all knew about it. It wasn't a well-kept secret. It was part of the buzz as it were. When shooting had finally ended, and we were at the wrap party, he made his move. We were in the parking lot and there were people everywhere. Still, he walked up to me, grabbed me, and kissed me passionately. Once our lips separated, I looked at him and said, "Oh my God." We started dating.

Later, but still early in the relationship, we were at his place kissing. He left the TV on. I asked him why it was still on and he said because he thought it created "pretty mood lighting." I said, "No, it doesn't." He said, "It is romantic, isn't it?" I was clear with him that it wasn't. There was nothing cute, pretty, or romantic about the glare of the TV. It was funny that he thought so, but not romantic. That night, which was early in the relationship, I vowed to keep my coat on the entire night to sort of maintain my virtue. In my attempt to be virtuous, all of the little ceramic pins on my coat ended up popping off that night. But I kept it on! Then I married him. That was twenty-five years ago.

I'll admit, there were lots of terrible and disastrous kisses, many of them work-related and many with famous people, so I should not talk about them, but I do understand the struggles of dating as much as anybody. I also remember these three amazing kisses, and the good news is that they help erase all of the missteps and bad dates and the stuff we laugh about.

Best Kisses Ever

I've had quite a few great kisses, but the one that edges out the others was with a guy I met at the Sundance Film Festival. We definitely had an undeniable chemistry from the moment we met. We were at a party. Throughout the night, he would find his way over to me and make small talk. It was sweet. Plus, he was quite handsome. More than that, he had a boyish glimmer in his eye that made me want to know more about him. A man with a boyish charm is hard to resist. When the festival ended, we continued to communicate by text for the next couple of weeks.

When we were both finally back in town at the same time, he took me to dinner. We went to Nobu in West Hollywood and enjoyed dinner and great conversation. There were many things that impressed me about him throughout the date. He was curious about me, but he also told me a lot about himself. By the end of dinner, I knew he was a quality guy. A good person. Big heart. Intelligent. Driven. And super sexy. It was a great first date. When he dropped me back at my place we both kind of sat in his car, neither of us moving. I kept my seat belt on, although I wasn't quite sure why. I think I was nervous, but in a good way. We chatted a bit as the tension mounted, and even though I don't normally kiss on a first date, there was no way I was going to turn him down if he went for it.

Not one second too soon, he went for it. He put his right hand gently through my hair and brought my lips close to his. He kissed me softly, but with purpose. His lips were soft and perfect. I kissed him back softly, too. He gently stroked my hair with his left hand. It was romantic and passionate. We sucked on each other's lower lips then he started with just enough tongue. I responded with mine. He led and I followed. It didn't feel rehearsed but it felt like we had been kissing for years: like we had perfected the kiss. I honestly could have kissed him all night. It was magical. We were in perfect sync and our chemistry couldn't have been stronger.

. . . .

As the kiss progressed, it got hotter and hotter. My seat belt did eventually come off but since it was a first date, I stayed in my seat and he was the perfect gentleman. Time seemed to stand still. When we finally ended the kiss, the windows were completely fogged. We had trouble parting our lips and kept going back for a little more. Despite my wanting to stay in his car, I knew without a doubt I would see him again. And I did. Each time after the kissing was just as good. I could have kissed him forever, and at one time I thought it could have been my last first kiss ever. —*Lindsay*

. . . .

I'd only been living in the United States for a year. My English was bad—I could only understand 30 percent of what people said. I was only fifteen. As in every high school, there was one super popular boy. He was handsome, more mature than his age, and every time he walked past girls, they would smile at him. He didn't know I existed. But his friend did and he always gave me his attention. The problem: Women don't want what's available, especially at that age. We want what everybody else wants. And most times it is what we can't have. Prom came around and the whole school was getting ready for it. Aurelio, the boy who liked me, asked me if I would be his date for the prom. I was so excited because if I went with Aurelio, that meant I would be going to the prom in the same car as the "man of my dreams," the guy every girl liked. I ran home and told my mom about it. Her response was, "Oy!" She sewed me a dress from black velvet, and I spent all day getting acrylic nails for the first time. Only the cool girls in school had those. I did my hair and makeup and painted on bright red lips. I waited anxiously by the door. When the limo finally pulled up I think I stopped breathing from excitement and nerves. My date came to the door and put a corsage on my wrist. We climbed into the car to find that the guy I liked had brought *three* girls with him. Hmm . . . not my kind of party. Everyone was laughing, drinking, and talking and I was trying to keep up with what they were saying. I was timing my laughs with theirs to try to cover up the fact that I had no clue what was happening. Before we arrived, the partiers wanted to play truth or dare. I had no idea what this was. I didn't even know what "dare" meant. When it was my turn, I just blurted out "Dare," hoping I pronounced it right. My dare was to seduce my date into a kiss. I was mortified. I had an out-of-body experience. I had no clue what I was going to do or how to even do it, especially in front of the guy I liked. Everyone got quiet and all eyes were on me. I decided to do a scene from a modern-day Cinderella story: *Pretty Woman*. Remember the scene in which she's watching *I Love Lucy* and eating strawberries? I got on my knees in front of him, heart pounding, and slowly and seductively slid my hand up his tuxedo trousers while slowly sliding my body up toward his chest. I put my hands on his chest and gently kissed his neck. At that point our faces were right in front of each other and I knew it was about to happen. He put his hand under my chin and led my lips to his and held that moment before finally locking lips. What happened next was an explosion of fireworks all around. My tongue found his, along with his Big Red gum. I had no clue if I was doing it right, but it sure felt amazing. The kiss lasted for what felt like an eternity and we didn't want to stop. We only did because the other guys started cheering and clapping. The kissing continued throughout the night, and from that point on the hot guy in school simply ceased to exist in my mind. At the end of the night, right before he dropped me off, he kissed me again, which smudged the red lipstick that I'd reapplied just minutes before all over my face. Oblivious and proud, I walked through the door to hear my mom say, "Well, it looks like you've had a great night!" —*Karina*

· ·

The best kiss I ever had took place on my wedding day. It was a beautiful kiss because it signified the beginning of something wonderful. Two kids later and almost ten years together, that kiss was the beginning of it all. It's still the best kiss I've ever puckered up for. —*Natalie B.*

· ·

My best kiss was after my first date with a guy I ended up dating for five years. It was unexpected and he went in for it so fast I didn't see it coming; we actually hit teeth it was so hard, but then it turned very, very intense! —*Natalie Y.*

. . . .

I was about eighteen-years-old, in my freshman year of college. He was my roommate's friend. After an early night of flirting, dancing, and of course, drinking, he finally kissed me outside the local, popular bar that everyone went to. The atmosphere around this kiss wasn't ideal, but the moment he planted one on me, no one else existed. Nothing else mattered. You could have thrown a pie in my face and I wouldn't have taken my lips off of his. We took the make-out session to the side of the building and then continued at the dorms after. He did leave me a parting gift: a big cold sore that hurt for days and left me housebound. It was all worth it, though. —*Melissa*

. . . .

My best kiss would definitely have to be the kiss I shared with the love of my life. Little did I know that that kiss was going to forever change my life. We went to dinner at BOA and came back to the house to make s'mores (he knew I loved them) and spend more time together. I was anxiously awaiting *the kiss* the entire night, and when I least expected it, he held my face and kissed me as a movie played in the background (I definitely didn't pay attention to what the screen was playing). He softly put his hand on my face to bring my lips in to match his. At first, it was just a kiss, but because our connection was so strong, it progressed really fast. It started off as a sensual kiss and then we started making out, tongue and all. It wasn't overbearing, like there was just enough tongue. A second later, the kiss became completely hot and heavy. When we kissed, it was so passionate, yet sensual and sexy. And yet, it was sweet. It was clear that in this one kiss, we had an undeniable connection and we didn't want it to stop. That kiss: The rest is history. —*Ivana*

. . . .

It was at one of those hip Hollywood clubs where there were too many people, it was impossible to hear, and everyone was trying just a bit too hard. Not exactly my scene but I had a few friends and a dance floor with my name on it. And then I saw him. It was almost as if time stood still in that room packed full of beautiful people. We locked eyes, smiled, and I looked away, thinking that's all it would be. Turns out, we had friends in common, and as he was introduced, he smiled, looked me in the eyes, and performed the requisite handshake. Electricity jolted through my body. He stood next to me and gently took my hand and we spent the rest of the night glued together. He was a curious creature and I was immediately intrigued. Not wanting to separate, we decided to grab late-night food. And as we left the restaurant, rain started to fall lightly and the streetlamps cast moody beams of light. He grabbed me in the middle of this quiet, tree-lined road, took my face in his hands, and kissed me. It was pure magic. —*Lesley*

. . . .

It was with my wife. She was the first real kiss, like the real deal. (Just one notch below a bleeding lip story.) I was definitely the greener of the two of us. It was kind of good and wonderful, except I didn't completely know what I was doing so I just kept doing it. We kissed and I didn't know when to stop, so I just kept kissing her. A car horn beeped and interrupted us; otherwise we'd still be there. Years later we laugh about how long that first kiss went on for. She said she was thinking, *are we done yet?* —*Ralph*

. . . .

Acknowledgments

There are so many people to thank for helping to make this book a reality.

Special Thanks from Karina

Thanks to my parents, Tatyana and Glen Smirnoff, who have inspired me with their love and taught me with their wisdom. Thanks for grounding me and protecting me.

And with profound gratitude, thanks to my best friend, my confidante, my sister from another mister, Lindsay Rielly. Thank you for always being there for me, for putting me in check when I deserved it, and for always giving me a shoulder to lean on. I love you!

To Stephanie Krikorian: Thanks for helping to get all of our crazy dates and stories onto the page and for working with us to make this a reality. It was a pleasure working with you. Here's to hopefully many more!

Thanks to the team at Post Hill Press, including Anthony and Michael. Anthony, you took a leap with this project and I'm grateful that you did. Also, thank you Lauren Brancato for the edits. We were moving quickly so we appreciate your eye.

Cheryl Burke: There is blood family you are born into, and then there is family you choose for life—the dancing family. We share a special bond with each other that I love and cherish with all my heart. Thank you for your input and your story! Cha-ching! The best $100 ever spent!

Lea Thompson: So glad to have met you and gotten to know you. Love listening to your stories and adventures. Thank you so much for making this book complete with your wisdom.

Ralph Macchio: To my brother from another mother, thank you for your patience, support, faith, and for always being in my corner. You're always brutally honest and I so appreciate that. Love you and the whole Macchio clan!

Ricardo Lauritzen: Besides the fact that you are an amazing hairstylist, you have also become my confidante. I come to you not only to get my hair done but to hear your opinions, assessments, and conclusions. Thank you for always being there for me!

Lisa Ann Walter: You are seriously the funniest person I've ever met. Witty, clever, intelligent, and absolutely gorgeous inside and out. This book would not be the same without you.

Jacoby Jones: After spending every day with you for almost four months and getting to know you, and seeing how protective and vigilant you are with me, your input in the book is so appreciated and valuable.

Obviously this book wouldn't have been possible without so many of you girls sharing your stories with us. You came forward to add to this book without hesitation and it's much appreciated. I love all of your attempts to flee restaurants or be nice to the duds you were out with while they starved you and acted weird. I love that you don't panic; you laugh about it all and still . . . keep looking. You'll find him. We all will. Here's to smiling while we do. Love you all. Thanks from the bottom of my heart.

Special Thanks from Lindsay

There are many people to thank for making this book possible. I'm not going to thank each disastrous date personally, since making the book is appreciation enough!

First and foremost, I want to thank my incredible son Royce who encourages me to be the best version of myself daily; who has taught me the value of time and how to quickly determine if someone is worth mine; who makes me laugh even through the storms . . . but most important, with his birth I learned that my capacity to love is far greater and deeper than anything I thought humanly possible. He has given me faith beyond question that all of these frogs will lead to "the one" at the perfect time. Royce, I love you more than the moon, the stars, and the sky, to infinity and beyond.

To my partner in crime, business, and adventure, Karina Smirnoff, for being the best co-pilot and best friend I could ever ask for. Thank you for trusting me with this book, for being one of the wittiest, most fun, good-hearted, beautiful, and wonderful people I know, and for taking this journey with me; through the ups and the downs we have remained true to each other. I will always be your biggest cheerleader, love you forever and always, be there to pick you up when you're down and celebrate with you all the triumphs life brings your way. I couldn't imagine making these memories without you!

Nancy and Keith Rielly, aka Mom and Dad, thank you for being the most amazing role models I could have asked for. I feel humbled that God gave me you guys as parents and confidantes. I never for a second take it for granted and know how truly blessed I am. I'm eternally grateful for your support and for helping me with Royce so I could go on many of these dates and follow my dreams! You guys are my rocks and have instilled in me qualities that make me proud of the woman I am today. Love you so much!

To my sister Lori Rielly, I'm so happy we finally get to let others laugh at your hilarious stories! As far back as I can remember, we have always been storytellers. That's what we did, and you were a pioneer in the documentary-style storytelling with classics like "Lindsay Talks." Thank you for always encouraging my craziness and for contributing to this project. All of our date-dishing was part of the inspiration for this book.

To my incomparable grandparents, Grandma Marianne and Grandpa John Hoyle, who are to this day two of my biggest cheerleaders. My grandma has always been my gossip partner— we've dished on many dates and relationships, plus many firsts and lasts. Your sixty-four years of wedded bliss inspire me and make me believe without a shadow of a doubt that all the disasters will eventually make me appreciate true love even more when I find it.

Thank you for being an example of how to love through sickness and in health forever and always. I love you both beyond measure.

Special thanks to Alex for being such a wonderful friend, partner in parenting, and father to our son. I'm blessed to have you in my life, and please only read the acknowledgments! Love you!

To Stephanie Krikorian, we couldn't have done this without you! From the start you have been an absolute gem. And a talented one at that! Our combined type-A personalities allowed us to accomplish what seemed like a far-fetched dream. You are a beautiful person inside and out, and when the right person walks into your life, he's going to be one lucky guy.

Anthony, thank you from the bottom of my heart for believing in the vision for this book. I know you put a lot of faith in me on this one, from the creative to the timeline. You trusted me implicitly and I appreciate you more than words can express. The journey has just begun, my friend. Thank you to Michael L. Wilson, Lauren Brancato, and the entire Post Hill Press team! We couldn't have wished for better partners on this book.

There are so many people who contributed to this book that I want to thank. Ladies (and gents), I promise these are in no particular order.

Lesley, we've been friends since third grade and have seen each other kiss many frogs. Thank you for always being such a wonderful, fun, honest, and amazing friend. And thank you for sharing a snapshot of your life in our book. I can't wait to see your happily ever after one day in the near future.

Mathis, I remember the last breakup and how devastated you were. Yet despite the tears you remained optimistic and faithful in finding love. And now to have found what all of us hope and pray for is so beautiful and beyond exciting. I can't wait to be in your wedding sooner than later and to continue on this journey together. Love you!

Melissa, you are the most difficult friend to discuss dating with yet you're spot on much of the time. Thank you for always making me laugh and for making me just that little bit more paranoid about the guys I date! Love you!

Kira, I adore you beyond words and can't believe what the past year and a half has brought you: the most amazing husband and your edible son Devon. What an inspiration your life is and a reminder of how quickly it can all change—for the better! Thank you for all the laughs. Love you!

Cheryl, it has been an absolute pleasure getting to know you over the years. You are a beautiful person, not to mention hilarious and a joy to be around. Thank you for enhancing our book with your amusing and envious story! Love ya!

Lea Thompson, thank you for contributing to our book. You give us hope that our happily ever after is out there and remind us to enjoy the journey, especially those unforgettable lip-locking moments.

Lisa Ann Walter, you are an absolute ray of sunshine. From the moment we met, we clicked. The night at the wedding takes the cake, despite there not being enough cake for us! You make everyone around you laugh and always inspire us to love ourselves and not settle for just any man. Thank you for your hilarious stories and for your friendship!

Thank you to my dear friends Ralph and Phyllis Macchio for being such unbelievable supports in my life. I adore you both and can only pray that I will find the kind of lasting love that you have found in one another. I love you both dearly. 12/24.

Ricardo, you are such a wise and wonderful friend. Thank you for always making me look my best and for being a constant and true friend. I love that many of the stories you've heard over the years have made it into this book. Your support means the world, thank you! Love you!

Jacoby Jones, my favorite #12 in the game! Thank you for always making Karina and me laugh and for looking out for us no matter what. Thank you for your hilarious insight in this book. Love ya!

I also want to thank Tanisha Thomas, who is the funniest person I know, who makes my dating life feel "normal," whom I love more than words can express.

To the fabulous and brilliant Michael Broussard for believing in us and our craziness and pushing us to get these stories out there!

Thank you to my wonderful friends: Leila Steinberg; DC Coleman; Jen Clyde; Collin Eckert; Angela Baker; Natalie Yuri; Kristi Cozens; Nicola Harrison; Natalie Bombet; Steven Ray; Jennifer Hart; Nino Paterson; Deena, Jerry, and Cami Katz; Randi and Morgan Geffner 12Forever; Ivana Steelman; Kevin Mann; Ray Luv; Martin Batstone; Steve Curliss; Jason Gibson; John Guglielmetti; Leah and Jeremy; Todd Krim; Bobby Montes; Yuka and Jay, Ai, Kai Oku; Desi, Dan, Reese, and Shea; goddess Dina; Laurie Muslow; Galit; Tatyana and Glen Smirnoff; Matty K.; Lizzie Grubman; Geneva Wasserman; Brenda Starr; my butterfly Maiele; Marilyn Wilson for being a genuine, funny, talented storyteller and incredible friend; and to Guiliana and Elizabeth whose brilliant stories enhanced our book.

To the rest of my family: Becky and Craig; Dan and Maggie; Janessa and Phil; Noah, Caleb, and Grayson. Randa and Bruce; Billy and Shawni; Tate, Tucker, and Ella; Karrie and Cory; Callan. Tom and Julie; Kristi and Kelly; Sierra and Jessica. George and Jenny; Jaclyn and Sean. Auntie Sandy and Uncle Bill; Kasey, Rielly, and Brady; Auntie Sue, Daryl, Bryanna, and Vanessa; Gwen; Kelly and Nick; Jade Robertson; John and Lesia Hambleton.

To my future husband—look at what I went through for you! And I'd do it all over again just to end up with you.

"And now these three remain: faith, hope, and love. But the greatest of these is love."
1 Corinthians 13:13.